Cruising the Canals
of the
Netherlands

2021 Edition

Tom Sommers

ISBN: 978-0983284123

Cover Photo: Dokkum, Friesland
City/town street map underlays courtesy of
©OpenStreetMap contributors
openstreetmap.org

EuroCanals Publishing
369 Montezuma Ave. Suite 154
Santa Fe NM 87501 USA
www.eurocanals.com
orders@eurocanals.com

About The Author

Tom Sommers, an American, began his canal-cruising avocation with a trip in 1966 aboard a classic wooden motorboat from Cayuga Lake, in the Finger Lakes of Central New York, through the New York State Barge Canal (Erie Canal) and the Oswego Canal to Lake Ontario and the St Lawrence River. Later canal trips included one across the length of the Erie Canal and down the Hudson River to the Statue of Liberty.

After early retirement from an engineering career, Tom moved to coastal North Carolina where he boated on the IntraCoastal Waterway and worked as a boat broker and as an advertising sales representative for a boating magazine, traveling the East Coast waterways from New York to Florida.

In early 2000 Tom and his wife Carol acted on a longtime desire to live in Europe and cruise the canals and rivers. Their first year was in Paris, on the Canal St Martin, then on the river Seine near Conflans-Ste-Honorine, and later on the northern coast of Brittany. During these years they have traveled extensively along the waterways and visited France, Belgium, Germany, the Netherlands, Luxembourg, Switzerland, Italy and England.

Beginning EuroCanals Publishing in September 2000 with the 8-page monthly newsletter "Cruising the Canals & Rivers of Europe", Tom currently offers e-book versions of waterway guides for France, Belgium, the Netherlands and Germany. EuroCanals maintains an extensive website describing the inland waterways of Europe at www.eurocanals.com

Previous books by Tom Sommers include the cruising guides:
Cruising the Canals & Rivers of France (2013/2018)
Cruising the Canals & Rivers of the Netherlands (2011/2018)
Cruising the Canals & Rivers of Belgium (2018)
Cruising the Canals & Rivers of Germany (2015/2021)
Orion - A Canal & River Cruise through Holland (2010/2020)
Cruising the Heart of Holland (2016)
Seine - From Sea to Source (2020)

At Tannay,
Canal du Nivernais, France

Cruising the Canals & Rivers of the Netherlands
2021 Edition

EuroCanals Guide: Heart of Holland was first published in November 2000 and expanded in 2005 to include all waterways in the Netherlands. The 2021 edition has been updated and expanded, with many more photos, maps and waterway data tables, with route suggestions to help in planning week-long trips. The guide provides information for travelers by barge, canal cruiser, bicycle, on foot or by car. It shows "Where You Can Go" and why you might want to go there.

The sections are arranged by geographical region, making it possible to view the connections between the waterways and thus plan a trip. Each canal or river has been assigned an identifying number (by the author) to assist in locating the waterways on the maps and tables. All waterways that are commonly used by private cruising boats have been listed on the maps and data tables, however some are shown on the maps and listed in the data tables but not otherwise described.

Included on many pages are website links to assist you in locating marinas and other mooring places, brokers for barges and canal cruisers, operators of self-skippered boat rental bases and various waterway authorities. More information is available from the EuroCanals website:
https://eurocanals.com

Many website links are included in this book; not all of them offer an English-language option. For those sites you can copy the relevant text and paste it into https://translate.google.com/
For more convenience and for translation of entire pages with one click, use the Google Chrome web browser or add a Translate extension to your Windows or Safari browser.

City and regional street maps are courtesy of OpenStreetMap contributors. These maps can be opened in a web browser to view more detail or a larger area; the detail shown for European towns and cities on these maps is much better than on the equivalent Google or Apple Maps.
Go to www.openstreetmap.org and Search by city or town name.

Using this book: The maps and descriptions included in this book are intended to provide useful information for planning cruises in the Netherlands and are not to be used for navigational purposes. Sources for suitable charts (ANWB/Waterkaarten) and a discussion on how to use them are shown on pages 105-108. The skipper of a cruising boat is solely responsible for obtaining and using the necessary charts and publications.

Table of Contents

Nederland: The Netherlands... low country

A flat country, about half of it lies below sea level, protected and reclaimed from the sea by dikes. A land of friendly people who speak a difficult language but communicate freely in English with visitors. While writing this guide I received an e-mail comment from an American owner of a Dutch canal cruiser:

> "Tom, we would highly recommend cruising Holland as a first taste of European cruising, because there are so many wonderful waterways which are far better maintained, buoyed and marked than our waterways in the USA. It's a great place to get your feet wet!"

The Netherlands has been a common starting point for many canal travelers over the past thirty years; they went there to find and purchase a barge or canal cruiser. But while some of them left quickly to go south to France or to return a new vessel to the UK, others have lingered or returned soon, drawn to the overwhelming presence of waterways, boats, boatyards, boat builders and reliable yacht brokers. Readers often contact me to ask for suggestions on a suitable spot to winter their boat while they return to their home country, or to select a competent boatyard to make repairs or renovations. Although there are many suggestions for these services in France and Belgium, it isn't surprising when they write back to say: "Thanks, but I think I will just return to Holland, there is a place that I know will fill my needs perfectly".

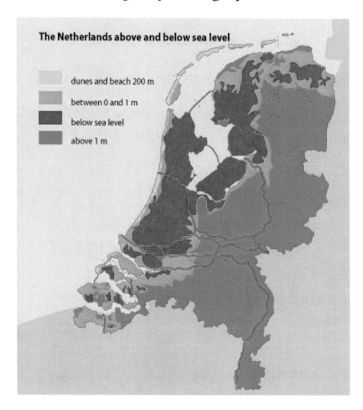

The Netherlands above and below sea level

dunes and beach 200 m

between 0 and 1 m

below sea level

above 1 m

Cruising is pleasant and navigating the waterways is easy. The waterways are used by some commercial traffic but the major canals and rivers are wide and it is easy for small boats to avoid the large barges. The canals are frequently several meters above the surrounding land and the fields below are flat, so the view is often panoramic and the feeling is one of gliding over the countryside. The surroundings are clean and maintained in the traditional Dutch style; nothing is left "lying about". Except for major electrical transmission lines, utilities are all underground and there is little to block the view except the trees along the banks. Elevation changes on the waterways are minor; locks are usually necessary only at the junctions of canals and rivers. Travelers can enjoy long stretches of uninterrupted cruising and occasional contact with the usually friendly and always efficient lock keepers.

The Provinces of The Netherlands

The Netherlands is often casually called "Holland" but in fact there are twelve provinces. It happens that the two largest cities, Amsterdam and Rotterdam, are in the two provinces named Holland (Noord and Zuid Holland respectively.) These provinces include most of the places that draw foreign tourists, hence the common usage of "Holland".

Noord Holland has two quite distinct parts: the bustling metropolitan and cultural area of Amsterdam and Haarlem, south of the east-west Noordzee Kanaal, and the rural peninsula stretching north to Den Helder. With the exception of the interesting and attractive city of Alkmaar, a cruise north on Noord Hollands Kanaal becomes progressively more lonesome and desolate. The canal follows closely alongside the straight-line highway, although there are other, smaller canals as an alternate route. The port of Medemblik, a pleasant town with good restaurants and a castle, is a favorite IJsselmeer stopover at the eastern end of these smaller canals.

Zuid Holland includes most of the country's commercial shipping harbors and industry; Rotterdam and the surrounding towns are also a good place to search for the purchase of a barge or cruising vessel. The northern part of the province, halfway between Rotterdam and Amsterdam, is prime cruising territory, a land of lakes, small canals and rivers through natural areas and historic towns such as Delft, Gouda and Leiden, described in this guide as the "Heart of Holland".

Zeeland has a very descriptive name, it is a province not far removed from the sea. Most of the land is protected from the North Sea by dikes and a complex system of dams. Over 1500 people died when the villages were inundated by the sea during a storm in 1953. Cruising in Zeeland is more properly in the category of coastal cruising rather than inland waterway travel; there is a great deal of open water which is tidal, with just a few canals cutting through islands and peninsulas. Vessels arriving from the English Channel can enter at Vlissingen, visit Middelburg and Veere, then connect with the inland waterways at the Volkerak. There are pleasant stopover ports at Willemstad and at Tholen on the inland route between Hollands Diep and Antwerp, Belgium.

Noord-Brabant is a large province with just a few canals. It includes the Biesbosch national park, a nature reserve of marshes and twisting channels, a favorite of those who enjoy mooring at a private island amidst wildlife. There are two canals from the northwest to the southeast of the province, as an alternate route from central NL to Maastricht, bypassing the north-flowing Maas river and its current.

Limburg is the long narrow strip of land on both sides of the Maas river, squeezed in between the hillsides of Belgium and Germany. Maastricht, the major city at the southern border, is well worth a visit. The river is picturesque and a enjoyable ride, with several useful ports along the way, as well as two recreational lakes just off the river.

Utrecht is both a city and a province. The city, the home of a major university, is a labyrinth of canals and rivers which penetrate the city center. The province includes many lakes, rivers and charming small towns. A cruise along the east-west Hollandse IJssel river or north-south on the very beautiful Vecht river would certainly be a highlight of a visit to Holland.

Gelderland is the largest province, spread across the middle of the country. The waterways are the *Grote Rivieren*, the "Great Rivers" of the Maas (Meuse) and the Waal (Rhine) and its branches. The primary rivers flow westward from the German border to the major cities of Rotterdam and Dordrecht. The IJssel river takes a solitary twisting line north to the IJsselmeer, a pleasant and popular route between Friesland and the cruising areas of Belgium and France.

OverIJssel includes a big chunk of land northeast of Gelderland, but the main boating area is the group of waterways at its western end between Zwolle, Meppel, Steenwijk and Blokzijl. In the center of this is Zwartsluis, a favorite services and long-term mooring port for many barge owners.

Flevoland consists of two below-sea-level polders. The town of Urk, once an island in the IJsselmeer, remains a major fishing port and has become a popular marina stop for cruisers.

Friesland is true boater's country; the residents have lived and worked by barge for hundreds of years and some remote farms can still be reached only by boat. A maze of canals and small channels connect dozens of "meers", filled with boats of all types during the summer months. The main highway for cruisers is the Prinses Margriet Kanaal, striking northeast from the IJsselmeer towards Groningen (and on to Germany and the Baltic Sea for some.)

Groningen continues the spread of small waterways across the flat plain of far northern Netherlands. The town of Delfzijl is the departure point from the inland waterways to the North Sea or Baltic, or to the inland waterways of Germany.

Drenthe is best known for the Drentsche Hoofdvaart, the canal from Groningen to Meppel/Zwartsluis and the waterways of central Holland, but it also connects to the "Turfroute" in southeastern Friesland. Skippers should also consider cruising in eastern Drenthe or on into Germany via connecting canals.

Comparing the Netherlands with France

France has arguably the most popular cruising waterways in Europe, but let's see how it compares to the Netherlands in numbers: the map at left shows the Netherlands (dark green) superimposed on France, at the same scale. France is 15 times larger in area.

One major numerical category is the number of bridges which must be opened for passage; this cannot be clearly shown as a number, since it depends on the air draft of each boat. In words in can be stated as:

> France = hardly any
> Netherlands = very many

Most of the bridges in France are fixed height; this permanently restricts the air draft of boats that may wish to travel those waterways.
For instance, the stone arch bridges of the Canal du Midi prevent quite a few motorboats, barges and certainly sailboats from using that canal. Without lifting bridges, there is no option.

In the Netherlands, the prevalence of lifting bridges means that tall boats can use all of the rivers and most of the canals, except those within the cities. In fact there are routes designated for travel by sailboats with masts up, the Staande Mast Route.

In Numbers:

	France	Netherlands
Number of Waterways	94	269*
Total kilometers	8,445	3,732
Total number of Locks	2,165	186**
Total number of Boats	Many	Too Many to Count

* These are the waterways that could be traveled by visiting cruisers; in addition there are hundreds, perhaps thousands, of small dead-end canals lined with boats and used by farms, residences and industry.
** The Canal de Bourgogne in France itself has 189 locks.

To be sure, numbers don't tell the whole story. The topography and culture of the two countries are quite different. Because of the topography, in France most of the canals use locks to climb up a slope alongside a river or over a summit between rivers; in the Netherlands, locks are generally needed only to adjust for tidal effects or flooding. The boating culture is entirely different; in France there are commercial barges and private boats used for leisure, while in NL boats of all types are simply everywhere and used by nearly everyone, for leisure, local transportation or work.

Grote Rivieren: The Great Rivers

The land of the Netherlands is the delta of two great north-flowing rivers, the Meuse and the Rhine; when they cross the border they become the Maas and the Waal. The river Rhine flows north in Germany then turns west as it crosses into NL. The main stream is the Waal; other branches are the north-flowing IJssel (Gelderse IJssel) and the west-flowing Nederrijn/Lek.

Brielle was formerly a port at the mouth of the Maas; silting has blocked the river and the town is now 2 km from the sea. The relative smoothness shown for the river lines in central NL, as compared to upstream, is accurate; the rivers have fewer and more gentle curves here, due to both the topography and to Dutch efforts at managing the rivers.

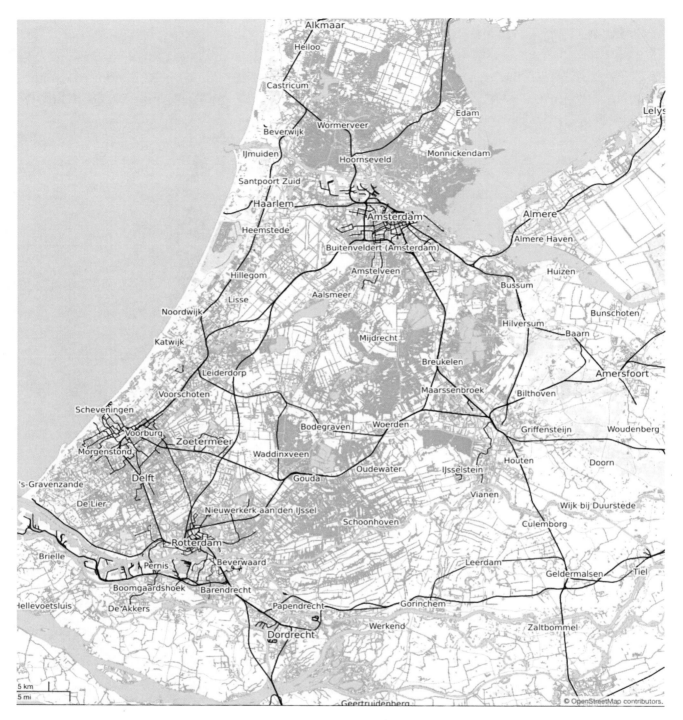

The map above clearly shows how much of Holland is under water (the black lines are railways.)
The provinces of Noord Holland, Zuid Holland and Utrecht have more water than they do dry land.
Of course, many of the lakes and canals are not suitable for navigation, as they are very shallow.
But there are more than enough navigable waterways to allow visitors to visit the towns and cities,
as well as reaching into the natural areas.

This map, as well as all background maps in this guide, are taken from Open Street Map, an open-
source website: www.openstreetmap.org. Go to that website, search by city name and zoom in.

The Inland Seas & Ports

Eight hundred fifty years after great floods of the 13th century inundated the land to form the Zuider Zee, the building of the Afsluitdijk in 1932 separated the saltwater Waddenzee from the freshwater IJsselmeer (the river IJssel flows from the Rhine into this great lake from the southeast, thus the name is IJssel-lake.)

Another dike, the Houtribdijk, divides the lake into a second inland sea, the Markermeer, named for the island of Marken. Close to Amsterdam the lower corner of the inland sea is named the IJmeer. Of the ports shown on this map Volendam, Hoorn and Hindeloopen have no inland access by canals. Locks at each end of the two causeways are double-acting, as the water level may be higher in either of the lakes at certain times.

The Inland Ports

Den Helder: Located at the northern end of the Noordhollands Kanaal, this is usually a port of entry or exit rather than a destination in itself. It is the main naval base of the Netherlands, thus most of the attractions and events are Navy-oriented. There is a great deal of warship traffic. The former Willemsoord Naval Dockyard has been converted to a marina for leisure boating, close to the center of town and with access from both the sea and the Noordhollandschkanaal.

Jachthaven Willemsoord www.willemsoordbv.nl 0223 61 61 00

Den Oever: This port offers convenient access to either the IJsselmeer or the Waddenzee, as well as inland waterways through Noord Holland to Alkmaar, Amsterdam or Haarlem. Marina Den Oever is located at the southwestern corner of the lock complex, near the end of the Den Oeversvaart. The small town offers some shops but few attractions.

Marina Den Oever www.marinadenoever.nl 0227 51 17 89

Medemblik: One of the favorite towns on the IJsselmeer; walk to the castle (with a moat), very nice town center with lots of restaurants and if you have bicycles go to the steam engine museum south of town. The inner harbor (Westerhaven) is between the lifting bridge and the lock (from the Westfriesche Vaart canal.) Pontoons are very convenient to the town center and within bicycle distance to a larger supermarket, ask the harbor master for directions.

Jachthaven Medemblik www.st-jachthavenmedemblik.nl 0227 54 18 61

Enkhuizen: This port offers convenient access to either the IJsselmeer or the Markermeer, however the inland waterway route is restricted to depths as low as 0.8-1.0m and height of 1.5m, on canals which connect to Medemblik. The town is another favorite stop, with sights from its days as the home base for the Dutch East Indies Company and the huge outdoor Zuiderzee Museum.

Havendienst Enkhuizen www.enkhuizen.nl 0228 31 24 44

Hoorn: Inaccessible via the inland waterways, this port offers modern shopping opportunities along with a great deal of historical sights and museums. There is a sheltered anchorage, two marinas and visitor's moorings at the Binnenhaven in the town center.

Havendienst Hoorn email: havendiensthoorn@planet.nl 0229 21 40 12

Grashaven Hoorn www.grashavenhoorn.nl 0229 21 52 08

Edam: Not surprisingly, the focus of this town is on cheese. In the summer there is a weekly market (Wednesdays) done in the tradtional manner. A marina (Jachthaven Galgenveld) and short-stay moorings are available near the Markermeer, with more moorings along the canal into the town.

Gemeente Werken Edam/Volendam (Nieuwe Haven) 0299 37 14 77 or 06 22 51 52 10

WSV De Zeevang/Jachthaven Galgenveld 0299 35 01 74

Volendam: Just south of Edam but accessible only from the Markermeer, this village is a popular tourist destination by land or by trip boat. Choose between a new marina away from town or municipal visitor's berths among the fishing fleet.

Marina Volendam www.marinavolendam.nl   0299 32 02 62

Gemeente Werken Edam/Volendam (Volendam Haven)   0299 39 83 98

Monnickendam: Sheltered behind Marken island, this port offers inland access to Amsterdam (depth 1.3m, height 3.9m) avoiding the busy Buiten IJ and Oranjesluizen. The town offers historic sights and an impressive row of traditional sailing barges. There are two marinas and two municipal moorings, the Binnenhaven (<12m) and the Gemeentehaven (>12m).

Gemeente Waterland www.waterland.nl 0299 65 55 67

Marina Monnickendam www.marina-monnickendam.nl 0299 65 25 95

Jachthaven Waterland www.jachthavenwaterland.nl   0299 65 20 00

Marken: Although connected to the mainland by a causeway, the island of Marken retains its traditional cottages and character, without becoming as touristy as the nearby mainland towns of Edam, Volendam and Monnickendam. Visitor's moorings are available, with water, electricity, toilets and showers.

WSV Marken 0299 60 13 82

Amsterdam: The river IJ is entered from the IJmeer via the Buiten IJ (outer IJ river) to the Oranjesluizen locks. Information regarding moorings is on page 44.

Muiden: This attractive upscale town is at the mouth of the river Vecht, offering access to central and southern Holland while bypassing the busy waters at Amsterdam or as an approach to Amsterdam from Muiden on the Muidertrekvaart.

Jachthaven Stichting Muiden   0294 26 12 23

Almere: There is a marina on the Markermeer (De Blocq van Kuffeler) however it is 4 km from town; the harbor was built as a refuge port. A better choice would be "around the corner" at Almere Haven on the Gooimeer, where more services are available nearby. Either of these ports allow access into the Flevoland polder on the Hoge Vaart or Lage Vaart.

Gemeente Haven Almere www.almere.nl 0365 38 22 37

Lelystad: There are marinas located on both sides of the lock complex, along with little-used visitor's moorings. Canals cross Flevoland polder to the northeast (to Ketelhaven), southwest (to Almere) or southeast (to Harderwijk.)

WV Lelystad www.wvlelystad.nl   0320 26 04 24

Jachthaven Lelystad Haven www.lelystadhaven.nl 0320 26 03 26

Ketelmeer: At the northern end of Randmeren van Flevoland, as it joins the southern edge of the Ketelmeer, two marinas are located outside the Ketelsluis. That lock provides access to the two canal routes into and across the polder: Hoge Vaart or Lage Vaart.

Inter Harbour Dronten www.interharbours.com 0321 31 82 37

Stichting Jachthaven Ketelmeer www.jachthavenketelmeer.nl 0321 31 22 71

Urk: A small picturesque working fishing village, this port is popular with some cruisers; others think it "smelly". The municipal harbor offers many berths with basic services. A canal connects across the Noordoostpolder to Blokzijl.

Gemeente Haven Urk email: havendienst@urk.nl 0527 68 99 70

Lemmer: A very popular water sport centre at the entrance of the Princes Margriet Kanaal. This is a main water highway taking large commercial barges from the Ijsselmeer through the north of Holland and on into Germany. There is a large commercial lock to the west of the town but for pleasure boats there is a lock to the south of the town centre. The town sits on either side of the Zijlroede, a separate canal which spurs off the Princes Margriet for pleasure boat traffic only. There are several marinas; the town is well served by shops and restaurants and a beach, along with two museums.

Gemeente Lemsterland Buitenhaven 0514 56 33 43

Gemeente Lemsterland Binnenhaven 0514 56 19 79

Jachthaven De Punt BV www.jachthavendepunt.nl 06 29 33 18 04

Stavoren: A historic seaport, today the town is a center for boatbuilders and service shops as well as a link directly into the center of the Friesland lakes. A north-south canal behind the town offers low-cost and convenient berths.

Gemeente Havenkantoor Stavoren 0514 68 12 16

Marina Stavoren Buitenhaven www.skipsmaritiem.nl 0880 50 41 20

Hindeloopen: An important center for sailing on the inland seas or the ocean and also a historic town, a major tourist destination. There is no direct access into the canal system, however Workum is just a few kilometers north on the coast.

Jachthaven Hindeloopen Buitenhaven www.skipsmaritiem.nl 0880 50 41 40

Workum: Another historic town and a gateway into the lakes and canals of Friesland, east to the Gaastmeer/Heegermeer or north to Bolsward.

Jachthaven It Soal www.itsoal.com 0515 54 14 43

Makkum: The first stop on the eastern shore of the IJsselmeer just inside the Afsluitdijk, Makkum is a delightful, compact fishing village. with plentiful shops and restaurants. There are sheltered municipal moorings inland of the sea lock and several full-service marinas along a 2km cut between barrier islands to the IJsselmeer. Canals connect to Bolsward and on to Sneek or south to Workum and Lemmer.

WSV Makkum www.wvmakkum.nl 0616 52 06 82

Marina Makkum www.marinamakkum.nl 0515 23 28 28

Harlingen: This is the customs port for vessels arriving from the sea and a major center for the sales and renovation of old barges. It is crossed by many canals; boats are moored everywhere. It is the western end of the major canal system which crosses Friesland from the North Sea to Germany passing through Franeker, Leeuwaarden and Groningen.

Noorderhaven/Zuiderhaven: Marina De Leeuwehbrug
jachthavenleeuwenbrug.nl   0517 41 56 66 Mobile 06 53 84 67 34

Map: Waterways of the Netherlands

Portals connecting the Netherlands with Belgium:

A - Terneuzen-Gent Kanaal provides a route south to Gent, allowing traffic to bypass Antwerp. It can be considered for passage between Holland and the coastal ports of Belgium across the relatively open waters of Zeeland, where caution is advised.

B - Schelde Rijnkanaal is an inland waterway between Holland and Antwerp via a sheltered bay at the eastern end of the Oosterschelde. Ports are available at Tholen or Bergen-op-Zoom NL. The waterway connects directly into the commercial docks of Antwerp and the pleasure-boat harbor in the center of the city.

C - Zuid-willemsvaart is a canal route into the northeast of Belgium, an alternative to the traffic and current of the Maas river. It is a useful connector from central Holland through the cities of Helmond and 'S-Hertgenbosch to Maastricht or westward across Belgium.

D - Maas river is a frequently traveled route from anywhere in the Netherlands into Belgium and on south to France. It is known as the Meuse river in Belgium and France. It also connects with western Belgium via the Albertkanaal.

Portals connecting the Netherlands with Germany:

E - Rhine river flows north across Germany, becoming the Waal in the Netherlands. It is a major route to all of Germany and the entire eastern, central and southern waterway network of France.

F - Rutenbrock canal connects from Ter Apel NL to Rutenbrock DE, where it becomes the Haren-Rutenbrock Kanal. It offers access eastward across Germany on the Mittelland Kanal or southward to the Rhine.

G - Emden is a port on the Dollard bay, across from Delfzijl NL. A canal leads eastward to Wilhelmshaven. The river Ems connects to Bremen, the Mittelland Kanal or southward to the Rhine.

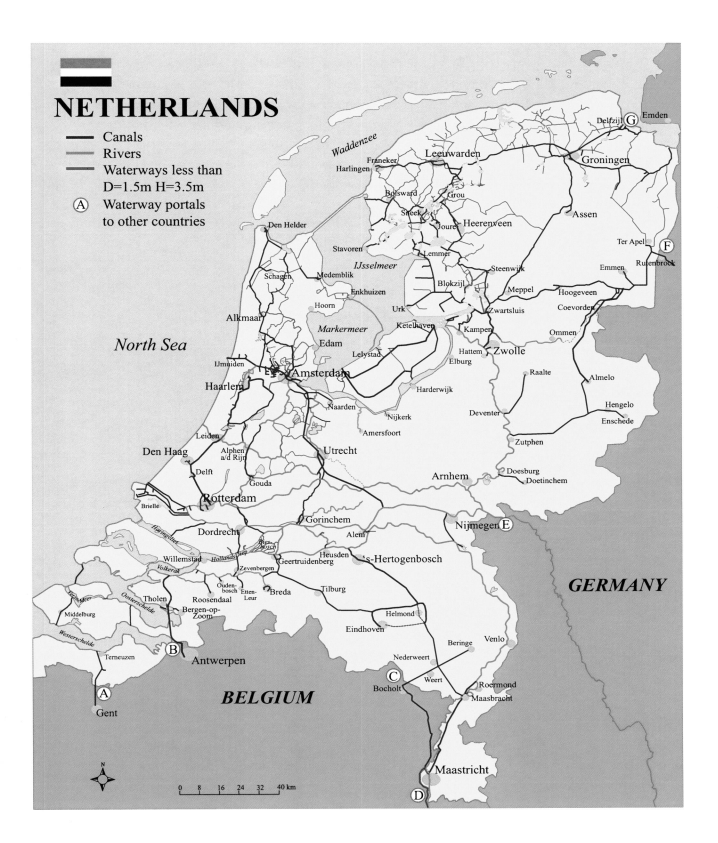

NETHERLANDS

— Canals
— Rivers
— Waterways less than
  D=1.5m H=3.5m
Ⓐ Waterway portals
   to other countries

North Sea

Waddenzee

IJsselmeer

Markermeer

Den Helder
Franeker
Leeuwarden
Harlingen
Bolsward
Grou
Sneek
Joure Heerenveen
Groningen
Delfzijl Ⓖ Emden
Assen
Ter Apel Ⓕ
Stavoren
Lemmer
Rutenbrock
Schagen
Medemblik
Steenwijk
Emmen
Enkhuizen
Blokzijl
Meppel
Hoogeveen
Hoorn
Urk
Coevorden
Ketelhaven
Zwartsluis
Alkmaar
Kampen
Ommen
Edam
Hattem
Zwolle
Lelystad
Elburg
Raalte
Almelo
IJmuiden
Amsterdam
Harderwijk
Hengelo
Haarlem
Naarden
Enschede
Nijkerk
Deventer
Leiden
Amersfoort
Zutphen
Den Haag
Alphen a/d Rijn
Utrecht
Delft
Arnhem
Doesburg
Gouda
Doetinchem
Rotterdam
Brielle
Gorinchem
Nijmegen Ⓔ
Haringvliet
Dordrecht
Alem
Bies-bosch
Heusden
's-Hertogenbosch
Willemstad
Hollandsdiep
Geertruidenberg
Zevenbergen
Volkerak
Tilburg
Zoommeer
Oudenbosch
Etten-Leur
Breda
Middelburg
Tholen
Roosendaal
Oosterschelde
Bergen-op-Zoom
Helmond
Eindhoven
Venlo
Westerschelde
Beringe
Terneuzen
Ⓑ
Nederweert
Roermond
Antwerpen
Ⓒ
Weert
Maasbracht
Bocholt
Ⓐ
Gent

GERMANY

BELGIUM

N

0 8 16 24 32 40 km

Ⓓ Maastricht

13

Using this guide

Tour Routes: A first glance at the map of the waterways in Holland can be confusing; it takes some study, and often suggestions from experienced cruisers, to pick out a suitable cruising route. This guide includes several suggested routes, each of which can be completed in one week of cruising. The routes are named by region and by the color which is used to show the suggested waterways on a map. These tours can be combined for longer cruises, and of course the schedule should be determined by the crew and skipper, stopping longer at favorite places. Use the waterway data tables for full details of the route.

Mooring Places: The descriptions in this guide mention various types of mooring places.

Passantenhaven	Translated literally, a harbor for passers-by; visitor's moorings which can range from a quay with no services to a full-service marina.
Gemeente (name)	Municipality responsible for moorings.
Jachthaven	Marina; may be commercial, club or municipality operator
WV, WSV	"Watersport Vereniging" water sport (yacht) club
WSC	"Watersportcentrum" water sport center, usually commercial operator
Jachtwerf	Boatyard, offering service, long-term (and possibly short-term) mooring

Telephone Numbers: The telephone numbers shown on these pages are those used for dialing within the Netherlands; that is, they start with 0. When calling from another country use the international country code 31 and then omit the first "0". Numbers beginning with "06" are mobile phones.

IJ: This combination of letters is used in many ways in the Dutch language. It is well known as the IJsselmeer and IJssel river, but there are also the cities of IJmuiden and Nijmegen, among other usages. It is pronounced "eye" or "ay" and is always indexed alphabetically as if it were the letter Y. Thus in the ANWB almanak IJmeer comes right after Yerseke and Nijkerk comes after Nuldernauw. Not knowing this small detail can lead to great frustration, when you are busy looking in the "I" section instead of "Y"!

Links: There are many Dutch-language website links shown; Google or other online services will translate them for you. These websites are useful for contact information and they often have many photographs.

Passantenhaven

Mooring quays for visitors (*passanten*) are often provided in the center of towns, managed by the local municipality. Fees and services vary widely, but the location is usually very convenient.

Gemeente Dongeradeel, Dokkum, Friesland

Town quay, Heerenveen, Friesland

BB Bridges

BB is the term used on charts; it stands for *beweegbare brug*, a bascule bridge which is hinged at one end and lifted by a pair of counterweighted arms. In some cases there is a bridge mechanism on each bank, so that the span is split in the middle and the sections lift to each side.

The sight of these arms standing above the countryside are more common than the windmills along the waterways. Most are graceful, some are utilitarian; newer bridges are often sculptural. Many different styles are shown in the photos throughout this book.

Bridges are plentiful along the waterways; they operate on a schedule with closed hours for lunch breaks and to allow the passage of road traffic, so it is important to plan ahead each day. Keepers operate the lifting bridges; however in many cases they are located remotely and operate via surveillance cameras.

Boaters should have small change handy because there is sometimes a charge of 4 to 6 euros to pass through the lock or bridge. Brug geld (bridge toll) and sluis geld (lock toll) is often collected the old-fashioned way, using a wooden shoe on a line from the bridge-keeper's pole.

Charts show the data for each bridge; the Van Leerbrug at Vreeland, shown above, is marked
BB H17.5-22 W92.9 763.

BB means beweegbare brug, a moveable bridge. H17.5-22 is the clearance under the closed bridge,
in decimeters, thus 1.7 to 2.20 meters, depending on the water level. Sometimes the passage can be
done without opening the bridge, as this barge can do, but most cruisers are 2.40 meters or more and
so need the bridge to open.

W92.9 is the width of the channel under the bridge, again in decimeters, thus 9.29 meters. 763 is the
identification number for this bridge. The VHF channel (if shown) allows radio contact with the
bridge-keeper (not required.) Bridges on the Vecht river are labeled KP wisselt, meaning that the
water level changes (see a discussion of the term KP on page 181.)

Not every bridge has a keeper on duty; a series of bridges may be operated using remote cameras.
Skippers should approach the bridge so that the boat is in the range of the cameras. Thus, the bridge
operator can see that there are ships that want to cross the bridge.

When approaching a fixed bridge it is obviously essential for the skipper to know the bridge height,
but it is also useful to know if the vessel can pass under a BB bridge without the need to have the bridge
opened; this is commonly done. A tutorial regarding bridge heights can be viewed on pages 178-183.

18

Molens (Windmills)

Windmills are a common sight along the waterways of Holland; hundreds are in the Heart of Holland area. They are marked by an icon on the navigational charts, so they make a good cruising landmark as well as being a pleasure to see.

Some are still in operation, especially those which have been preserved in groups as museums.

Full details on the name, location and history of each molen can be found on this database: www.molendatabase.nl/nederland/

ANWB Charts

ANWB is the Royal Dutch Touring Club. In addition to maps for highways, they publish charts and brochures for the inland waterways in NL; these charts are essential for navigation. The charts are entirely in Dutch; if you buy the charts in person you should ask for a Legend brochure, which describes the items shown on the map in English. The charts are water-resistant, printed on both sides. There are 21 charts, see map on next page.

The charts have recently been updated and revised. Some of the features include detailed maps of the most important ports and full information about marinas, berths, buoys, depth of the waterway, fuel points of sale, maximum speed and bridges/locks dimensions.

The important items to look for are the depth of each canal and the clearance required to pass under fixed bridges. A careful study of the chart will allow you to decide if your vessel can navigate a particular canal (you will, of course, need to know the dimensions of your vessel; be sure to take note of the draft (depth), beam width) and air draft (minimum height above water.) The dimensions on the charts are shown in decimeters, so can be a little tricky at first. For instance, the Demmerikse Sluis (lock) is labeled "D22 W65 L295"; therefore it is 2.2 meters deep, 6.5 meters wide and 29.5 meters long. The bridge nearby is labeled "H38 W175", or 3.8 meters height by 17.5 meters width. A confusing label is a headroom marked H27,5 (with European style decimal point) meaning 27,5 decimeters = 2.75 meters.

ANWB also publishes an annual "Wateralmanak Vaargegevens" (Waterways Almanac) that covers both Netherlands and Belgium. "Deel 1" (Volume 1) describes regulations and certificate requirements and is required to be kept onboard all vessels.
"Deel 2" provides detailed information on waterways, bridges, locks, marinas, authority contacts, etc. Both of these books are in Dutch.

The charts and the Wateralmanak 2 are intended to be used together. Operating schedules for locks and bridges can be looked-up in the "Nummer kunstwerken" pages at the back of the almanac, using a reference number taken from the chart; this will refer you to the page in the almanak, where it is part of a waterway or town description. Some towns will include a detailed local map.

There are many VVV offices located throughout the Netherlands, most of which will sell the charts for their local area. Marinas, chandlers and even general bookstores may have the charts. But for pre-planning a trip and for peace of mind it is best to order the appropriate charts in advance from online services. To buy online from countries outside NL go to: https://www.vaarwinkel.nl
Zoek/Search for: ANWB Waterkaarten
Be sure to add the free "Legenda voor ANWB Waterkaarten".

ANWB Charts

The charts are identified by number and name, as shown on this map:

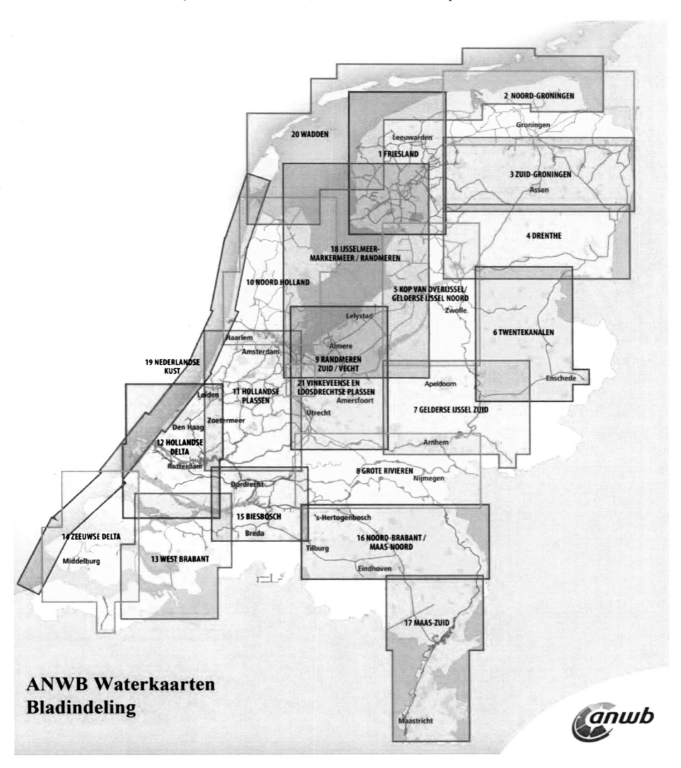

ANWB Waterkaarten
Bladindeling

Digital Charts for phone/tablet

A very convenient and relatively inexpensive way to use interactive charts onboard, or for planning your route, is to install in an iPad, iPhone or Android device the "Waterkaarten" app.
Originally this was a digital copy of all ANWB paper charts, assembled into a single page; Biggerworks Nautical Maps has now expanded it to include all of the Netherlands, Belgium and Germany for a seamless display of all navigable waterways in those countries.

To get the app go to the app store on your device and search "Waterkaarten" or "Biggerworks"; you will get several results, be sure to look for the one shown at right on an iPhone:

The app displays a single page map of the entire region; enlarge the screen to zoom in on the area of interest, with the added convenience of pop-up windows displaying the dimensional details and operating schedules of marinas, locks and bridges.

It is a very large file size, it will take many minutes to install when on wifi. For offline use, download individual sections of the chart as needed; they will consume a significant portion of the storage available on the device. A brief trial is free, then you can subscribe by month (€12.99), season (€29.97) or year (€42.99). For more information: https://waterkaarten.app

The app displays symbols for marinas, locks and bridges (zoom in on the app to show the symbols; the numbers 1,2,3,4 in this example mean there are more than one symbol underneath the icon.) Tap on a symbol to open a pop-up link to a page with details of that location. Skippers should use this feature regularly while cruising to check on the current bridge & lock operating schedule.

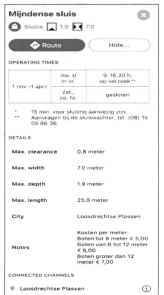

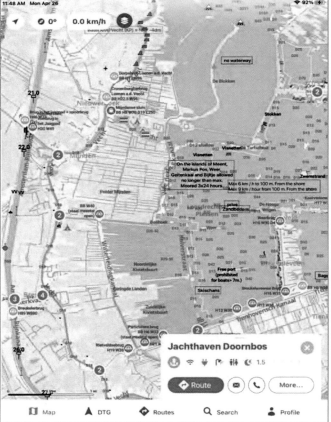

Staande Mastroute

Sailboats or tall motoryachts (height greater than six meters) can navigate along an inland waterways route through the Netherlands, avoiding the open sea. There are numerous bridges but all of them will open on schedules that have been coordinated by the various waterway managers.

At Amsterdam the "night convoy route" is traveled by groups of boats passing northbound or southbound on the Kostverlorenvaart between the Nieuwe Meer and Houthaven, at the Noordzeekanaal. Passages begin after midnight; a transit fee is charged. (See Amsterdam map pg 75)

"ANWB Wateratlas Staande Mastroute" is a 48-page booklet with full details of the complexities of this route.

To purchase online, go to: www.anwb.nl/ and search (zoek): Wateratlas Staande Mastroute.

Dutch traffic light system for locks and opening bridges

Passage through locks and opening bridges is controlled by red/green traffic lights; this system is used throughout the Netherlands. The lights are controlled by an operator on the scene or watching a video link, and occasionally by an automatic system triggered when a boat passes a photoeye.

Hagesteinsluis, on the river Lek near Vianen

During closed hours each panel will show two red lights (each panel shown includes three lights: two red/one green.) During opening hours they show a single red light. DO NOT ENTER, even if the gates are open or bridge is up.

When they are ready to open each panel will show one red plus a green light, indicating that they are about to open. When the red light goes out and only the green is showing you are clear to proceed.

It is important not to enter a lock or go under a bridge, even if it appears clear, if only one red and no green light is showing. This is telling you that boats on the other side of the lock or bridge have priority and you must wait for them.

Not in operation

Do Not Enter

Opening Soon

Enter now

Hatenboer base, Neuwegein

Locaboat penichette, from Loosdrecht base

Jachtverhuur
(Yacht For Hire)

"Do visit Holland as a captain on your own ship! You will not regret it. Our boats are easy to sail."
A quote from Mr. van de Laan of P. A. v. d. Laan Yachtcharter, in his brochure. They are not only
easy to sail, they are also well maintained, reliable and clean. You can be confident in the equipment
and services provided by the companies listed on the regional pages. Websites of these companies
are comprehensive and are themselves a guide to the waterways of the Netherlands; you will find
photos and descriptions of the available boats as well as booking information and suggested routes.
See pages 44 and 115 for locations and websites of many yacht rental bases.

P.A. Van der Laan base, Woubrugge

Waterway Maps & Dimensions

Detailed maps and dimensional details of the waterways of the Netherlands are presented in four regions, shown on the following page. The waterways are indexed by number on each regional map and in the column titled "Map" on the data tables which follow.

Waterway Names: There are hundreds of names used on these waterways; the name often changes every few kilometers, based on references to the local area. In some cases these changes are ignored on the data tables, where they have been grouped under a common name for the entire distance between the "From" and "To" points.

Map No.: These are index numbers which have been assigned by the author, for the purpose of identifying the waterways without trying to fit long names on the sometimes crowded map pages. These numbers have no relation to ANWB charts.

Km Long: The overall length of the waterway in kilometers.

From & To: Nearby place names (town or city) are used unless the waterway intersection is isolated, then the name of the connecting waterway is used.

Number of Locks & Lock Size: The number of locks along the waterway does not include floodgates (keersluis) which normally stay open (when they are closed there is no passage.) Locks which normally stay open but will be used when water levels require it are included. The length and width of locks may vary along the waterway. Lock Size shown is the minimum length and minimum width, not necessarily on the same lock. These dimensions, along with Draft & Height, are the limiting factors which may restrict the use of that waterway by a specific vessel.

Draft & Height: Some of these waterways are rivers; many are affected by tides or seasonal variations. Water levels may vary substantially, causing large variations in water depth and bridge clearances. Great care should be taken in planning and executing a trip. Contact local authorities and gather information from bridge and lock-keepers, other boaters and barge captains. "Open" means that there are no bridges along the waterway. "BB" means a beweegbare brug, an opening bridge; when a dimension such as "BB2.1" is shown, that is the clearance under the closed bridge or an adjacent passage. Fixed bridges are described as vaste brug; it is the clearance under such bridges that is shown in the Height column.

Dimensions: Dimensions are shown in meters; on the ANWB charts and books they are in decimeters (tenths of a meter.)

PLEASE NOTE:

Regional Maps: The author has divided the country into four regions; each region is shown on an enlarged map, with appropriate data tables for that region. In order to present the maps and data tables in an easily-readable size, these pages have been turned 90°, from portrait to landscape format, and enlarged to full-page size. Each map is therefore at a different scale; the relative sizes of the regions can easily be seen on the index map, at right. A kilometer scale is included on each map.

NETHERLANDS

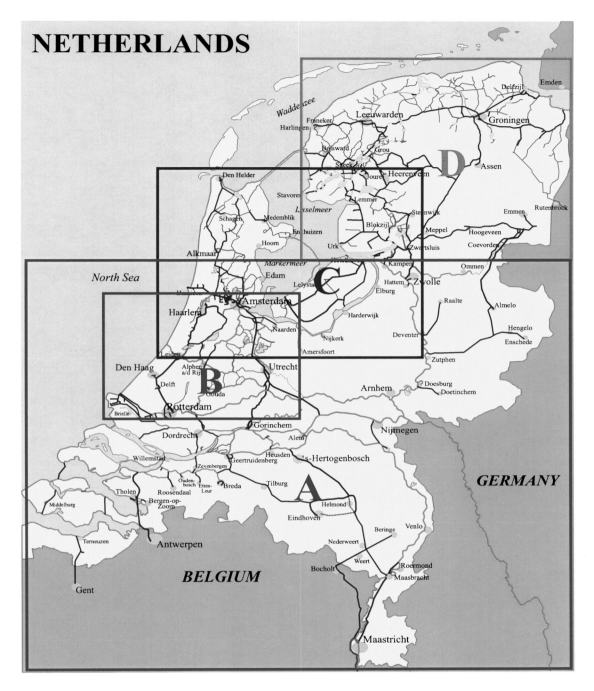

Regional Maps:
Region A - page 28
Region B - page 40
Region C - page 97
Region D - page 109

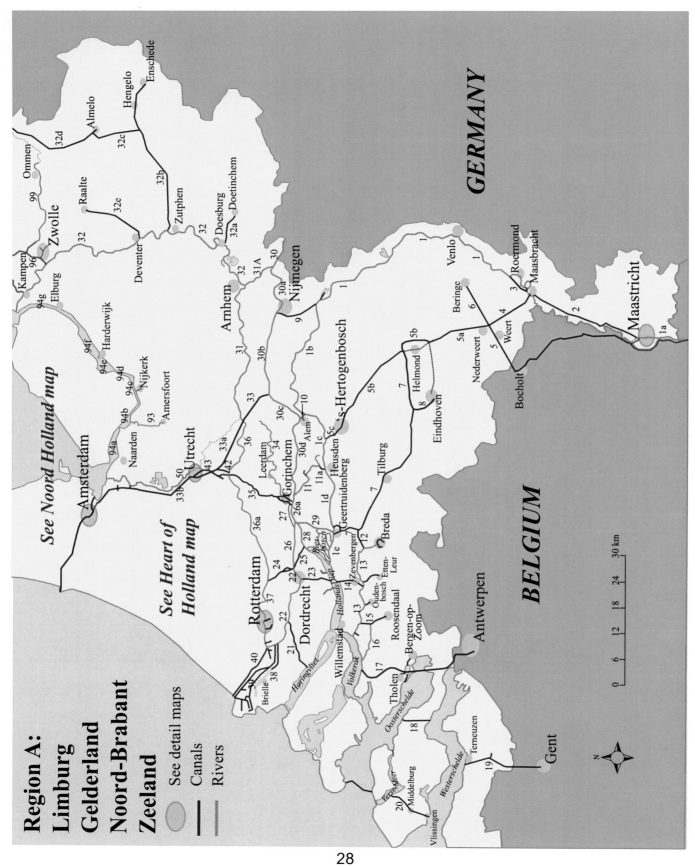

Region A:
Limburg
Gelderland
Noord-Brabant
Zeeland

See detail maps
—— Canals
—— Rivers

See Noord Holland map

See Heart of
Holland map

GERMANY

BELGIUM

N

0   6   12   18   24   30 km

28

WATERWAY	MAP	FROM	TO	KM LONG	No. of LOCKS	LOCK SIZE	DRAFT	HEIGHT
Maas (river)	1A	Lanaye BE	Julianakanaal	6.5	0		3.0 m	7.0 m
Maas (river)	1	Maasbracht	Maas-Waalkanaal	94.0	4	14.0X142	2.7	8.5
Maas (river)	1B	Maas-Waalkanaal	Kanaal St Andries	43.0	2	14.0X110	3.0	9.1
Maas (river)	1C	Kanaal St Andries	Heusden	21.0	0		3.6	10.6
Bergse Maas (river)	1D	Heusden	Geertruidenberg	21.0	0		3.6	9.0
Amer (river)	1E	Geertruidenberg	Hollandsdiep	11.3	0		5.0	open
Julianakanaal	2	Maastricht	Maasbracht	35.0	3	14.0X136	2.8	6.8
Lateraalkanaal Linne-Buggenum	3	Maas river	Maas river	7.3	1	16.0X142	2.8	10.9
Kanal Wessem-Nederweert	4	Maas river	Nederweert	16.0	1	7.2X145	2.8	5.0
Zuid-Willemsvaart	5	Bocholt, Belgium	Nederweert	18.5	4	7.5X63	2.1	5.1
Zuid-Willemsvaart	5a	Nederweert	Helmond	20.0	4	9.6X82	1.90	5.30
Zuid-Willemsvaart	5b	Helmond	's Hertogenbosch	37.0	6	6.9X50	2.30	5.50
Dieze (river)	5c	's Hertogenbosch	Maas river	6.1	1	13.0X90	2.80	5.80
Noordervaart	6	Nederweert	Beringe	15.0	1	n/a	1.65	5.00
Amertak/Wilheminakanaal	7	Amer river	Zuid-Willemsvaart	73.0	4	7.5X65	1.90	4.90
Donge (river)	7a	Bergse Maas	Zuid-Willemsvaart	3.0	0		3.30	5.6
Beatrixkanaal	8	Wilheminakanaal	Eindhoven	8.4	0		1.90	5.00
Maas-Waalkanaal	9	Maas river	Waal river	13.0	2	16.0X260	3.00	8.50
Kanaal van St. Andries	10	Maas river	Waal river	1.5	1	14.0X110	4.00	9.30
Andelse Maas (Afgedamse Maas)	11	Heusdenskanaal	Waal river	14.5	1	13.0X100	2.90	7.35
Heusdenskanaal	11a	Maas river	Andelse Maas	1.5	0		3.80	11.40
Markkanaal	12	Mark river	Wilheminakanaal	4.5	1	14.0X120	2.50	7.00
Mark & Dintel (rivers)	13	Volkerak	Breda	35.0	1	12.0X115	2.60	7.00
Roode Vaart (north)	14	Hollands Diep	Zevenbergen	6.0	0		2.40	open
Roode Vaart (south)	14	Zevenbergen	Mark & Dintel	2.0	0		2.10	
Mark-Vlietkanaal	15	Mark & Dintel	Roosendaal	10.0	0		3.50	7.00

WATERWAY	MAP	FROM	TO	KM LONG	No. of LOCKS	LOCK SIZE	DRAFT meters	HEIGHT meters
Steenburgse Vliet/Roosendaalse Vliet	16	Volkerak	Mark-Vlietkanaal	16.0	2	7.9X66	2.40	open
Schelde-Rijnkanaal	17	Volkerak	Belgium border	37.0	1	24X325	4.00	9.10
Kanaal door Zuidbeveland	18	Oosterschelde	Westerschelde	9.0	1	24X280	4.80	7.50
Kanaal Gent-Terneuzen	19	Westerschelde	Belgian border	14.0	1	18X140	13.50	open
Kanaal door Walcheren	20	Verse Meer	Westerschelde	14.5	2	n/a	3.70	open
Spui	21	Haringvliet	Oude Maas	15.0	0		3.00	open
Oude Maas	22	Beneden Merwede	Nieuwe Maas	30.0	0		5.00	6.90
Dordtse Kil	23	Oude Maas	Hollands Diep	10.0	0		8.00	open
Noord	24	Beneden Merwede	Lek river	13.0	0		4.80	6.60
Wantij	25	Nieuwe Merwede	Beneden Merwede	7.4	1	7.3X43.0	2.10	3.60
Beneden Merwede	26	Werkendam	Papendrecht	14.3	0			10.50
Boven Merwede	26a	Gorinchem	Beneden Merwede	6.0	0			12.50
Kanaal van Steenenhoek	27	Beneden Merwede	Gorinchem	8.9	1	6.3X31.6	2.50	2.90
Nieuwe Merwede	28	Beneden Merwede	Hollandsdiep	19.0	0			open
Steurgat	29	Nieuwe Merwede	Bergse Maas	6.0	1	7.0X55.4	2.20	4.50
Bovenrijn (upper Rhine river)	30	German border	Pannerdenskanaal	10.0	0			open
Waal (Rhine river)	30a	Pannerdenskanaal	Maas-Waalkanaal	19.0	0			14.10
Waal (Rhine river)	30b	Maas-Waalkanaal	Amsterdam-Rijnkanaal	26.5	0			14.20
Waal (Rhine river)	30c	Amsterdam-Rijnkanaal	Kanaal St Andries	13.0	0			open
Waal (Rhine river)	30d	Kanaal St Andries	Gorinchem	30.0	0			17.00
Pannerdenskanaal	31A	Waal river	Gelderse IJssel river	10.5	0			open
Neder-Rijn	31	Gelderse IJssel river	Amsterdam-Rijnkanaal	50.0	2	18.0X260	3.00	12.50
Gelderse IJssel (IJssel) river	32	Neder-Rijn	Ketelmeer	118.0	0		3.00	5.30
Gekanaliseerde Oude IJssel	32a	Doesburg	Doetinchem	12.0	1	7.8X55.0	2.50	6.00
K. Zutphen-Enschede (Twentekanaalen)	32b	Zutphen	Enschede	10.0	3	n/a	2.80	6.00
K. Zutphen-Enschede (Twentekanaalen)	32b	Zutphen	Enschede	10.0	3	n/a	2.80	6.00

WATERWAY	MAP	FROM	TO	KM LONG	No. of LOCKS	LOCK SIZE	DRAFT meters	HEIGHT meters
Zijkanaal naar Almelo	32c	K. Zutphen-Enschede	Almelo	3.0	0		2.50	6.00
Kanaal Almelo-De Haandrik	32d	Almelo	Coevorden	39.0	3	n/a	1.90	6.50
K. Deventer-Raalte (Overijssels Kanaal)	32e	Deventer	Raalte	3.0	1	12.0X105	2.50	6.00
Amsterdam-Rijnkanaal	33	Waal river	Nederrijn/Lek	72.0	1	18.0X350	6.00	9.00
Amsterdam-Rijnkanaal	33a	Nederrijn/Lek	Merwedekanaal	72.0	1	18.0X350	6.00	9.00
Amsterdam-Rijnkanaal	33b	Merwedekanaal	Amsterdam	41.0	0		6.00	9.00
Linge (river)	34	Gorinchem	Geldermalsen	35.0	1	W5.0	1.80	5.00
Merwedekanaal (south of Lek)	35	Gorinchem	Lek river	24.0	2	12.0X120	2.80	7.20
Merwedekanaal (north of Lek)	35a	Lek river	Amsterdam-Rijnkanaal	5.0	2	12.0X120	2.80	6.70
Merwedekanaal (north of Amstdm-Rijnk.)	35b	Amsterdam-Rijnkanaal	Vaartse-Rijn	1.0	1	12.0X120	2.80	6.40
Lek (river)	36	Amsterdam-Rijnkanaal	Lek Kanaal	21.0	1	18.0X220	6.00	13.00
Lek (river)	36a	Lek Kanaal	Noord river	40.0	0		6.00	13.00
Nieuwe Maas	37	Noord river	Oude Maas	24.0	0		6.00	10.50
Brielse Meer/Voedingskanaal	38	Oude Maas	Brielse	14.0	1	7.5X68.2	2.50	3.60
Hartelkanaal	39	Oude Maas	Europoort/North Sea	18.0	0		11.00	5.20
Nieuwe Waterweg	40	Oude Maas	North Sea	22.0	0		13.00	open
Hollandse IJssel (river)	41	Nieuwegein	Oudewater	19.0	0		1.70	4.40
Hollandse IJssel (river)	41a	Oudewater	Gouda	13.0	1	6.0X24.5	1.90	4.90
Hollandse IJssel (river)	41b	Gouda	Nieuwe Maas	17.0	1	24.0X120	4.00	BB
Lekkanaal	42	Lek river	Amsterdam-Rijnkanaal	6.0	1	18.0X220	3.50	9.10
Vaartse Rijn	43	Merwedekanaal	Vecht river	2.0	0		3.00	3.30
Vecht (river)	50	IJmeer at Muiden	Loosdrechtse Plassen	22.0	1	7.6X48.0	2.10	4.00
Vecht (river)	50a	Loosdrechtse Plassen	Utrecht	18.0	1	8.1X82.5	1.50	4.00
Eem river	93	Eemmeer	Amersfoort	18.0	0		3.00	7.20
Zwarte Water	96	Zwarte Meer	Zwolle	22.0	0		3.30	5.50
Overijsselse Vecht	99	Zwarte Water	Junne near Ommen	33.0	2	6.0X36.0	1.70	3.30

Maas River

While there are other canal routes into Belgium and on to France, the Maas/Meuse river is the main north-south route for many boaters. Current from the northward flow is low enough that it can be conquered by almost any motor vessel and the wide river means that avoiding the commercial traffic is not a problem. There are adequate moorings along the Maas, however charts should be used to plan ahead. Popular stops are Maastricht, Roermond (8 marinas) and Venlo, as well as the Leukermeer and Mookerplas lakes.

Connecting waterways to the other major rivers are: Maas-Waalkanaal (#9), leading to the Waal, Nederrijn or IJssel; Kanaal van St Andries (#10), a 1.5 km link between Maas & Waal; Andelse Maas (#11), a 16 km link between the Maas and Waal.

The flow in the Maas (#1a-d) has been tamed by a lock at the Belgian border, a bypass canal (Julianakanaal, #2) with 3 locks and another six locks on the Maas below Maasbracht. The Waal river (the Dutch part of the Rhine, #30a-d) and the IJssel (#32) are open, no locks at all and the current is faster. The Nederrijn (#31) branch of the Waal has two locks; the current is similar to the Waal.

The current in each river will vary with the season and with the amount of rainfall in each watershed; "normal" flow rates are:

Maas/Meuse	3-5 km/hr
Waal & Nederrijn	4-6
IJssel (normal)	5-6
IJssel (high water)	7-8

The Maas can be bypassed completely by utilizing the Wessem-Nederweert (#4) & Zuidwillemsvaart (#5) route or Wilhelminakanaal (#7). These canals offer leisurely but not very interesting travel.

Maastricht

The historic heart of this most European city in the Netherlands is a few blocks south from the Oude Bassin; first the Markt square, then Vrijthof, a large square with cobblestones, bordered by cafés and restaurants, is dominated by two churches: St.-Servaaskerk and St.-Janskerk.

Nearly all of the streets in the area bounded by the Markt square, Vrijthof and the river are pedestrianized, narrow cobblestone alleys. The few streets in this zone which do allow traffic do not have space for parking; the area is wonderful for wandering about, to view the preserved buildings. Cafes with open-air tables are scattered throughout these streets, just as they are at Vrijthof and at the Bassin.

The St Servaas bridge is a massive stone bridge, with seven identical arches and one wide flat span at the eastern shore, over the channel designated for barge traffic. It is widely regarded as the oldest bridge in the Netherlands; construction began in 1280, to replace a collapsed Roman bridge. To the south, upstream, is the Hoge Brug; a modern steel arch supports a suspended footbridge in a single 153 meter span over the entire river. The well-located marina 't Bassin www.tbassin.nl can be entered from the Maas via Sluis 20 or from the Zuidwillemsvaart via Sluis 19.

Free moorings are available along the wall in the center of the river between the St Servaas and Wihelminabrug bridges; barges follow the channel on the eastern side.

Other full-service marinas are located on the Maas, just to the south of the city.

Central Holland - Brown Tour

This circuit is primarily a river tour: westbound on the river Lek, south on the Noord and Wantij, east on the Nieuwe and Boven Merwede; these are all branches of the Rhine and Maas rivers. The final leg is north on the Merwedekanaal. The direction was selected to minimize the effect of current in the rivers. The tour can be done in the opposite direction. An alternate return can on the Hollandse IJssel river in case the westward flow of the Lek river is too strong or if the rental boat is not permitted on the Lek.

There are two excursions shown below, both are highly recommended: A day-trip on the Linge river to Leerdam and return offers a pleasant cruise on a slow, twisting stream through a countryside of green fields and meadows dotted with dairy cows.
Or continue on the Linge to Geldermalsen for an overnight.

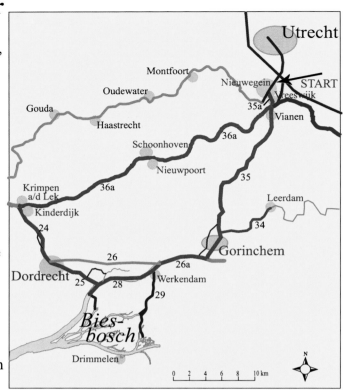

Biesbosch National Park is a green maze of rivers, islands and a vast network of narrow and wide creeks. The area is one of the largest natural areas in the Netherlands; it is one of the few remaining freshwater tidal areas in Europe. Visitors can pass through on the main channels or spend time exploring the small streams and wetlands by canoe or dinghy.

WATERWAY Names are as shown on ANWB charts	FROM	TO	KM	LOCKS	BRIDGES to open	DEPTH minimum	WIDTH locks/ bridges	HEIGHT fixed bridges	TRAVEL TIME hours
Merwedekanaal	Nieuwegein	Vianen	3.0	1	3	3.1	9.0	none	
Lek river	Vianen	Krimpen	38.3	0	0	2.0	155.0	13.5	
Noord river	Krimpen	Dordrecht	9.4	0	0	4.8	43.0	6.6	
Day 1		**Dordrecht**	50.7	1	3	2.0	9.0	6.6	6.0
Wantij	Dordrecht	Ottersluis	8.2	1	2	2.0	10.7	4.4	
Nieuwe Merwede	Ottersluis	Spieringsluis	2.0	1	0	4.4	6.0	none	
Gat van de Hardenhoek	Spieringsluis	Biesbosch	2.0	0	0	2.3	open	none	
Day 2		**Biesbosch**	12.2	2	2	2.0	6.0	4.4	2.0
Steurgat	Biesbosch	Werkendam	6.5	1	1	2.5	7.0	4.5	
Boven Merwede	Werkendam	Gorinchem	8.0	1	0	5.0	4.4	12.5	
Day 3		**Gorinchem**	14.5	2	1	2.5	4.4	4.5	3.0
Linge river	Gorinchem	Leerdam	16.0	1	3	2.7	7.9	5.2	
Linge river (alternate)	Leerdam	Geldermalsen	22.0	0	0	2.0	5.0	5.0	
Day 4		**Geldermalsen**	16.0	1	3	2.7	7.9	5.2	3.0
Linge river	Geldermalsen	Arkel	33.0	0	0	2.0	5.0	5.0	
Merwedekanaal	Arkel	Vianen	18.0	1	7	2.6	8.0	7.2	
Merwedekanaal	Vianen	Nieuwegein	3.0	1	3	3.1	9.0	none	
Day 5		**Nieuwegein**	54.0	2	10	2.7	8.0	5.0	5.0
TOTAL			125.4	8	19	2.0	4.4	4.4	19.0

Central Holland - Brown Tour

Nieuwegein: This modern city was selected as a starting point because of its location at the junction of the Amsterdam-Rijnkanaal and the Merwedekanaal and also because it is the home of Hatenboer Yachting, one of the largest rental-boat fleets in the Netherlands. Visitor moorings are available along the Merwedekanaal.

     Hatenboer Yachting www.hatenboer.nl 06 29 34 11 51

Vreeswijk: An historic barging center because of its central location, the town lies on the north bank of the river Lek. The old canal, (right) now with no access to the river, passes through the center of town, a very pleasant stroll with classic bridges and sidewalk cafes. Water traffic now uses the new Merwedekanaal on the west side or the even newer Lekkanaal on the east. Classic barges can be seen along the canals; a barging museum has recently been created. www.museumwerf.nl

Passantenhaven Vreeswijk
06 11 25 65 24

Nieuwpoort: A well-preserved fortified town directly on the south bank of the Lek, this is an interesting short stop for a return to the 17th century. The Buitenhaven (outer harbor) and Binnenhaven (inner harbor) canal is no longer in use but it provides a walkway through the center of town; return via the dikes of the star-shaped walls along the Singel (moat.)

     WSV Nova Portus 0184 60 12 46

Schoonhoven: Just across the river on the north bank, this is the historic "Silver Town" of the Netherlands. Shops and craftsmen are located throughout the old district, especially in the Watertower, an interesting and often-photographed building. Free moorings are offered nearby (no facilities, 1 meter tide) and a modern marina is a short distance east.

     Gemeente Schoonhoven (Noordhaven) 06 48 13 18 33

     Jachthaven 't Wilgerak   0182 38 28 36

Kinderdijk/Krimpen a/d Lek: At the junction of the Lek and the Noord rivers, Kinderdijk is the largest group of old windmills in NL. The 19 molen were built around 1740 to drain the polder. There is no mooring on the south bank near the site but there are two marinas on the Krimpen side and a ferry for access.

     WV Smit Kinderdijk 06 22 11 42 27

     WV De Lek 0180 52 47 21

Dordrecht: This city offers several marinas but, more importantly, it is a center for boat services. It is located at a 4-way rivers intersection: the Oude Maas, Noord, Beneden Merwede and Wantij. There are numerous haven areas; Nieuwe Haven is centrally located. From the tower of the nearby Grote Kerk there is a view of the rivers and cities.

Marinas: KDR&ZV Nieuwe Haven   0786 13 39 05   VHF31

               WSV Drechtstad 2 locations: Vlijhaven & Wijnhaven 0786 14 28 25

               WSV 't Wantij   Wijnhaven

               WSV Maartensgat Maartensgat   www.maartensgat.nl   0786 13 10 53

               Watersportbedrijf De Graaff   Wantij   www.degraaffwatersport.nl   0786 13 23 19

Services: Jooren Scheepsschroeven (propellors) Beneden Merwede

                   www.joorenscheepsschroeven.nl_ 0786 13 38 31

               De Groot Scheepstechniek Dordrecht Beneden Merwede

                   www.degrootscheepstechniek.nl 0786 16 55 99

               Kemper en Van Twist Diesel   www.kvt.nl   0786 32 66 00

               Hartog en Zn. (propellors) Beneden Merwede

                   www.hartogscheepsschroeven.nl   0786 14 82 19

KDR&ZV (Royal Dordrecht Rowing & Sailing Club) is located at Nieuwe Haven, adjacent to the Grote Kerk, Dordrecht. It is a very popular marina in the heart of the old city.

Biesbosch national park and nature preserves: The Biesbosch (rush woods) is one of the national treasures of the Netherlands, a large area of waterways between wooded islands, farmland and sandy beaches. Several preserves are set aside for birds. Along with canoes, kayaks and tour boats, motorboats are welcome (speed limit 9 km/hr in channels, 6 km/hr elsewhere) and can find many moorings or anchor for up to 3 days. You don't need to speak Dutch for this notice on the chart: *Biesbosch verboden voor jetskies en waterscooters*.

The three sections (see map on next page) Dordtse Biesbosch, Sliedrechtse Biesbosch and Brabantse Biesbosch were divided in 1870 by the creation of the Nieuwe Merwede canal, connecting the waters of the Waal river with those of the Maas. Two locks, Ottersluis and Spieringsluis separate the smaller channels from the river flow; many visiting boaters cross between these locks, sometimes causing long waits on summer weekends. At Spieringsluis, in the center of the Biesbosch, and at Drimmelen, on the south side of the Amer river, marinas offer docks with services and rentals of kayaks, canoes and small motorboats for an intimate way to travel through the park.

www.jachthavenoversteeg.nl/bootverhuur.php

bootverhuurdrimmelen.nl

Marinas: WV De Biesbosch Drimmelen www.wsvbiesbosch.nl 0162 68 22 64

Jachthaven Biesbosch jachthavenbiesbosch.nl 0162 68 22 49

WV De Amer www.wvdeamer.nl 0162 68 27 88

Jachthaven Van Oversteeg Spieringsluis www.jachthavenoversteeg.nl 0183 50 16 33

WSV Werkendam www.wsvw.nl 0183 67 84 21

Jachthaven De Steur www.jachthavendesteur.nl 0183 50 10 57

Boatbuilders: Zijlmans Drimmelen www.zijlmans.nl 0162 68 25 41

De Scheepsbouwers Maritiem www.descheepsbouwers.nl 0183 50 32 91

Service: Scheepswerf Van der Hoeven www.scheepswerf-vdhoeven.nl 0162 68 50 08

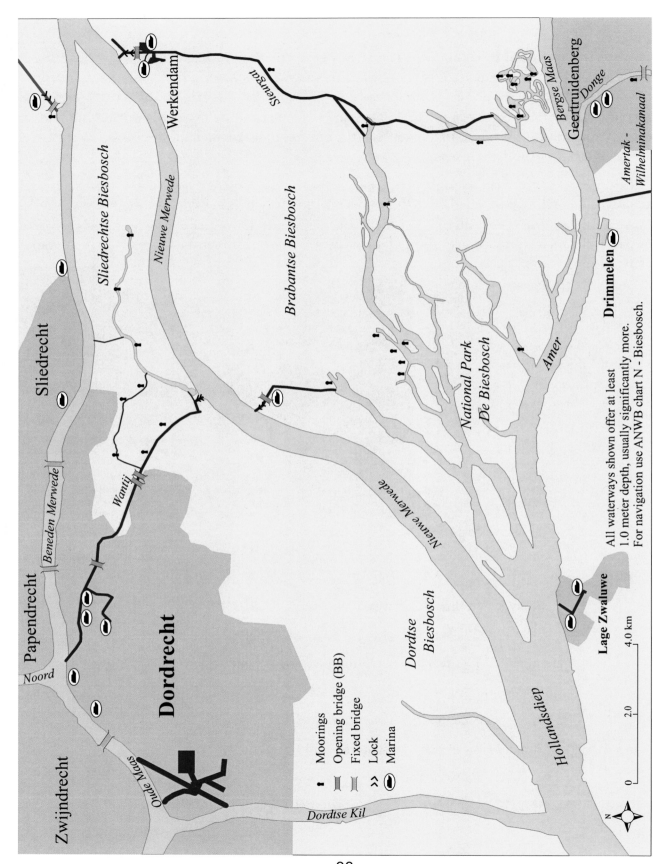

Papendrecht

Zwijndrecht

Sliedrecht

Werkendam

Sliedrechtse Biesbosch

Nieuwe Merwede

Beneden Merwede

Noord

Wantij

Dordrecht

Oude Maas

Dordtse Kil

Dordtse Biesbosch

Brabantse Biesbosch

Steurgat

Bergse Maas

Geertruidenberg

Donge

Amertak - Wilhelminakanaal

National Park De Biesbosch

Amer

Drimmelen

Nieuwe Merwede

Hollandsdiep

Lage Zwaluwe

All waterways shown offer at least
1.0 meter depth, usually significantly more.
For navigation use ANWB chart N - Biesbosch.

Moorings

Opening bridge (BB)

Fixed bridge

Lock

Marina

0   2.0   4.0 km

N

Gorinchem   This is a popular city for waterway travelers, both because of its location and its services. It is a major waterway junction on the Boven Merwede/Waal river (the name of the river changes from Waal to Boven Merwede at the Andelse Maas junction, 2.5 km east of Gorinchem.) The Merewedekanaal is an important route north to Utrecht and Amsterdam. There are two good marinas within walking distance of restaurants and shops, as well as a fully-stocked chandler near the Lingehaven. The river Linge is a very pleasant cruise, north and east to Leerdam and Geldermalsen.

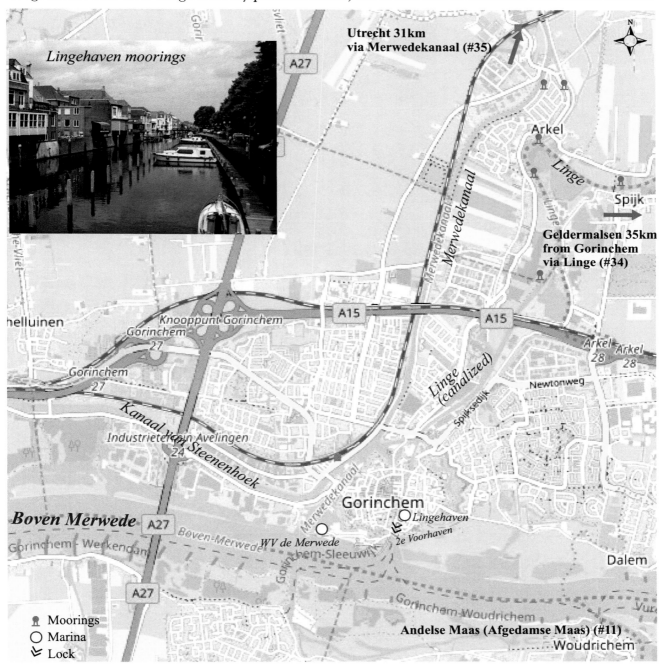

Lingehaven moorings

Utrecht 31km
via Merwedekanaal (#35)

Arkel

Linge

Spijk

Geldermalsen 35km
from Gorinchem
via Linge (#34)

A15

A15

Arkel
28

Arkel
28

helluinen

Knooppunt Gorinchem
Gorinchem
27

Newtonweg

Gorinchem
27

Linge
(canalized)

Kanaal van Avelingen
Industrieterrein Avelingen
24

Steenenhoek

Gorinchem

Boven Merwede   A27

Boven-Merwede

WV de Merwede

Lingehaven
2e Voorhaven

Dalem

Gorinchem - Werkendam

Gorinchem-Sleeuwij

A27

Gorinchem-Woudrichem

♟ Moorings
○ Marina
⩊ Lock

Andelse Maas (Afgedamse Maas) (#11)
Woudrichem

WV de Merwede   www.wvdemerwede.nl   018363 16 97 / 06 53 72 64 83
Lingehaven   www.lingehavengorinchem.nl   0183 65 93 14

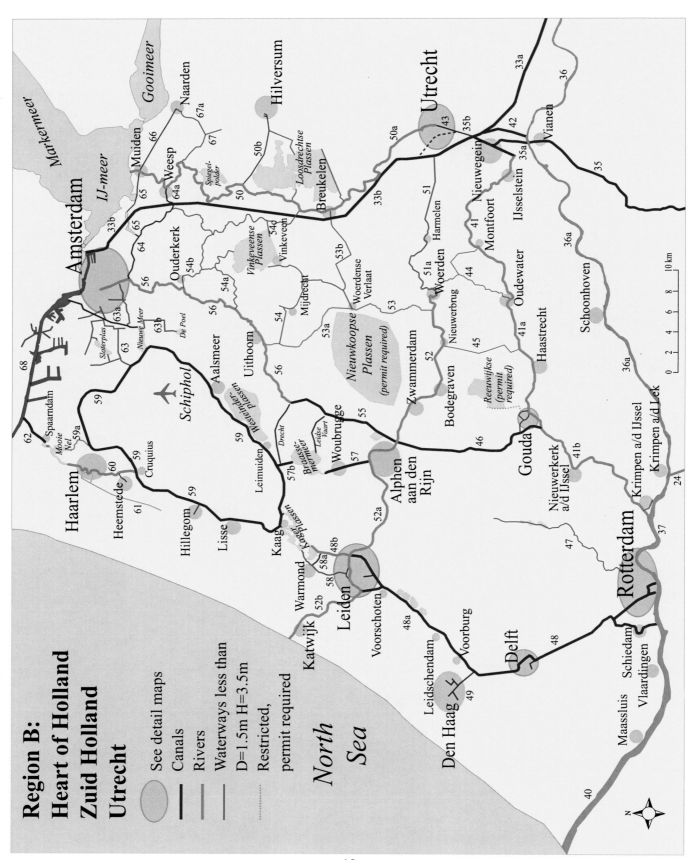

Region B:
Heart of Holland
Zuid Holland
Utrecht

See detail maps
Canals
Rivers
Waterways less than
D=1.5m H=3.5m
Restricted,
permit required

North
Sea

Markermeer
Gooimeer
IJ-meer

Amsterdam
Haarlem
Heemstede
Hillegom
Lisse
Kaag
Warmond
Katwijk
Leiden
Voorschoten
Leidschendam
Voorburg
Den Haag
Delft
Schiedam
Vlaardingen
Maassluis
Rotterdam
Gouda
Nieuwerkerk a/d IJssel
Krimpen a/d IJssel
Krimpen a/d Lek
Schoonhoven
Haastrecht
Oudewater
IJsselstein
Montfoort
Nieuwegein
Vianen
Utrecht
Woerden
Harmelen
Bodegraven
Nieuwerbrug
Zwammerdam
Alphen aan den Rijn
Woubrugge
Uithoorn
Mijdrecht
Vinkeveen
Ouderkerk
Aalsmeer
Breukelen
Hilversum
Naarden
Muiden
Weesp
Spaarndam
Cruquius

Schiphol

Nieuwkoopse
Plassen
(permit required)

Reeuwijkse
(permit required)

Loosdrechtse
Plassen
Vinkeveense
Plassen
Spiegel-
polder

Westeinder plassen
Brasse-
mermeer
Leidse
Vaart
Drecht
Kaagplassen

Nieuwe Meer
De Poel
Sloterplas
Mooie
Nel

Woerdense
Verlaat

62 68 63 63a 63b 56 64 65 33b 64a 65 66 67 67a 50b 50 50a 35b 33a 36
59a 59 60 61 59 59 57b 58a 58 52b 48b 52a 48a 49 48 40 37 24 36a 35 35a 42
52 53b 54a 54b 54 54c 53 53a 52 51 51a 44 41 45 41a 41b 47 46 55 57 43

WATERWAY	MAP	FROM	TO	KM LONG	No. of LOCKS	LOCK SIZE	DRAFT meters	HEIGHT meters
Amsterdam-Rijnkanaal	33	Waal river	Nederrijn/Lek	11.6	1	18.0X350	6.00	9.00
Amsterdam-Rijnkanaal	33a	Nederrijn/Lek	Merwedekanaal	19.1	1	18.0X350	6.00	9.00
Amsterdam-Rijnkanaal	33b	Merwedekanaal	Amsterdam	41.3	0		6.00	9.00
Merwedekanaal (south of Lek)	35	Gorinchem	Lek river	24.0	2	12.0X120	2.80	7.20
Merwedekanaal (north of Lek)	35a	Lek river	Amsterdam-Rijnkanaal	5.0	2	12.0X120	2.80	6.70
Merwedekanaal (north of Amstdm-Rijnk.)	35b	Amsterdam-Rijnkanaal	Vaartse-Rijn	1.0	1	12.0X120	2.80	6.40
Lek (river)	36	Amsterdam-Rijnkanaal	Lek Kanaal	21.0	1	18.0X220	6.00	13.00
Lek (river)	36a	Lek Kanaal	Noord river	40.0	0		6.00	13.00
Nieuwe Maas	37	Noord river	Oude Maas	24.0	0		6.00	10.50
Nieuwe Waterweg	40	Oude Maas	North Sea	22.0	0		13.00	open
Hollandse IJssel (river)	41	Nieuwegein	Oudewater	19.0	0		1.70	4.40
Hollandse IJssel (river)	41a	Oudewater	Gouda	13.0	1	6.0X24.5	1.90	4.90
Hollandse IJssel (river)	41b	Gouda	Nieuwe Maas	17.0	1	24.0X120	4.00	BB
Lekkanaal	42	Lek river	Amsterdam-Rijnkanaal	6.0	1	18.0X220	3.50	9.10
Vaartse Rijn	43	Merwedekanaal	Vecht river	2.0	0		3.00	3.30
Linschoten	44	Oudewater	Woerden	10.0	1	3.8X15.0	0.60	2.00
Wiericke	45	Hekendorp	Nieuwerbrug	8.0	1	4.4X33.0	1.70	1.80
Gouwe/Gouwekanaal	46	Gouda	Alphen a/d Rijn	14.0	1	12.0X110	2.80	7.00
Rotte river	47	Rotterdam	Rottemeren	10.0	0		1.20	2.50
Delftse Schie	48	Rotterdam	Delft	9.0	0		2.50	6.80
Rijn-Schiekanaal/Delftse Vliet	48a	Delft	Leiden	25.0	1	7.0X70.0	2.50	5.60
Zijl	48b	Leiden	Kager Plassen	6.0	0		2.50	4.90
Trekvliet (Den Haag)	49	Rijn-Schiekanaal	Den Haag	2.0	0		2.80	open
Vecht (river)	50	IJmeer at Muiden	Loosdrechtse Plassen	22.0	1	7.6X48.0	2.10	4.00
Vecht (river)	50a	Loosdrechtse Plassen	Utrecht	18.0	1	8.1X82.5	2.10	4.00
Hilversum Kanaal (vessels <12m)	50b	Vecht river	Hiversum	8.0	0		2.60	4.50

WATERWAY	MAP	FROM	TO	KM LONG	No. of LOCKS	LOCK SIZE	DRAFT meters	HEIGHT meters
Leidse Rijn (river)	51	Amsterdam-Rijnkanaal	Harmelen	6.0	0		1.50	2.40
Oude Rijn	51a	Harmelen	Woerden	5.0	1	3.1X17.5	2.00	1.90
Oude Rijn	52	Woerden	Aarkanaal	12.0	1	5.6X40.0	2.20	2.60
Oude Rijn	52a	Aarkanaal	Leiden	11.0	0		2.50	4.60
Oude Rijn	52b	Leiden	Katwijk	10.0	0		2.50	BB
Grecht	53	Woerden	Woerdense Verlaat	10.0	1	5.1X31.0	1.50	open
Kromme Mijdrecht	53a	Woerdense Verlaat	Amstel river	11.0	0		2.10	BB
Heinoomsvaart/Geer Bijleveld/Grote Heicop	53b	Woerdense Verlaat	Breukelen	10.0	0		1.40	BB
Kerkvaart/Ringvaart van Groot Mijdrecht	54	Kromme Mijdrecht	Vinkeveense Plassen	11.0	1	4.3X17.5	1.00	2.50
Oude Waver/Waver	54a	Amstel river		9.0	1		1.20	BB
Winkel	54b	Waver	Vinkeveense Plassen	1.5	1	5.2X22.0	1.20	BB
Bullewijk	54c	Vecht river	Waver	3.0	0		2.20	3.80
Holendrecht	54d	Bullewijk	Abcoude	3.0	0		1.30	2.80
Aarkanaal	55	Oude Rijn	Amstel river	11.0	0		2.50	5.60
Amstel (river)	56	Aarkanaal	Amsterdam	26.0	0		2.30	5.80
Heimanswetering/Woudwetering	57	Alphen a/d Rijn	Braassemermeer	4.0	0		2.80	open
Oude Wetering	57b	Braassemermeer	Ringvaart	1.0	0		2.50	open
Haarlemmer Trekvaart/Leede	58	Leiden	Kager Plassen	4.0	0		1.50	1.90
Grote Sloot	58a	Leede	Zijl	1.0	0		2.00	open
Ringvaart van de Haarlemmermeerpolder	59	Aalsmeer	Aalsmeer	60.0	0		2.50	4.70
Buiten Liede/Binne Liede	59a	Ringvaart	Mooie Nel	1.0	0		2.50	1.00
Spaarne	60	Ringvaart	Haarlem	9.0	0		2.70	BB
Liedse Tekvaart	61	Haarlem	Bennebroek	10.0	0		2.50	2.00
Zijkanaal C	62	Spaarndam	Noordzeekanaal	4.0	1	12X100.9	3.50	BB

WATERWAY	MAP	FROM	TO	KM LONG	No. of LOCKS	LOCK SIZE	DRAFT meters	HEIGHT meters
Slotervaart	63	Ringvaart	Sloterplas	3.0	1	7.5X41.8	2.50	2.10
Kostverlorenvaart	63a	Nieuwe Meer	Noordzeekanaal	4.0	1	12.0X120	3.20	BB
Hoornsloot	63b	Nieuwe Meer	De Poel	2.0	0		1.00	1.90
Weesper Trekvaart	64	Amstel river/Omval	Amsterdam-Rijnkanaal	9.0	0		2.10	4.95
Smal Weesp	64a	Amsterdam-Rijnkanaal	Vecht river	2.0	0		2.10	BB
Muidertrekvaart (max 4m X 12m)	65	Amsterdam-Rijnkanaal	Vecht river at Muiden	4.0	0		1.10	BB
Naardertrekvaart (max 4m X 12m)	66	Vecht river at Muiden	Naarden	7.5	1	4.9X26.0	1.10	BB
s-Gravelandse Vaart	67	Vecht river	dead end	4.0	1	4.9X26.5	1.20	BB
Karnemelk-sloot	67a	s-Gravelandse Vaart	Naarden	2.0	0		1.00	1.10
Noordzeekanaal	68	Amsterdam-Rijnkanaal	IJmuiden	24.0	1	11.0X110	3.50	open

Nes aan den Amstel

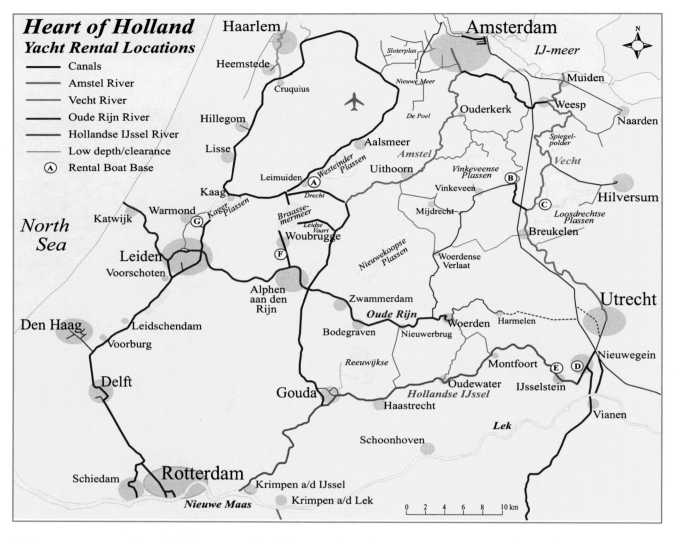

It is easy to rent a boat (15 meters or less) for a cruise of one, two or more weeks on the waterways of Holland. A brief checkout of the boat and a lesson at the base will acquaint the skipper and crew with the operation of the boat and the rules of the road for the waterways to be traveled.

Once underway, the skipper is in full control of the itinerary. Each day of travel can be as short or as long as desired, with stops for dining, sightseeing, and overnight stays usually decided as you go. Some of the companies operate more than one base, thus the cruise can be one-way or round-trip, back to the starting point. You may moor along the bank in the canals or anchor in lakes. You'll find marinas with shore power and other services. Small charges may apply.

MAP CODE	COMPANY	TOWN	WEBSITE	TELEPHONE at base
A	Waterfront Jachtcharter	Aalsmeer	www.jachtcharter.com	+31 (0) 111 672 890
B	Le Boat	Vinkeveen	www.leboat.com	
C	Locaboat	Loosdrecht	www.locaboat.com	+31 (0) 294 237 742
D	Hatenboer Yachtcharter	Nieuwegein	www.hatenboer.nl	+31 (0) 629 341 151
E	Delos Yachtcharter	IJsselstein	www.delosyachtcharter.nl	+31 (0) 626 146 301
F	Yachtcharter Van der Laan	Woubrugge	www.laanyacht.nl	+31 (0) 172 518 113
G	Olympia Charters	Warmond	www.olympia-charters.nl	+31 (0) 713 010 043

Heart of Holland

Fine old cities, windmills, bulbfields, dairy cows and water everywhere...

... define the image of the Heart of Holland. The lakes region of the provinces of Noord Holland, Zuid Holland and Utrecht includes extensive polder landscapes, canals, rivers, natural areas, forests and open-water lakes, all connected by waterways.

"Everywhere you look it's like a 17th century Dutch painting. It's all church steeples, windmills, cows and canals." That was the comment of a passenger on a recent trip along the maze of waterways that make up the Heart of Holland. She could have also included a comment on the more modern additions: "...boats by the hundreds and thousands, and vast fields of greenhouses and flowers."

Surrounded by a ring of major cities and lots of commerce and industry, the region that Dutch tourism and environmental groups call the "Groene Hart" (green heart) retains a natural and traditional ambience. It includes portions of the provinces of Noord Holland, Zuid Holland and Utrecht, however it is mostly in Zuid Holland (South Holland) and is often referred to by that name. Although it measures less than 40 km in diameter on a map, it is an ideal location for a cruise of a week or even more. There are so many waterways to explore and interesting cities and villages accessible from those waterways that a week is hardly enough time.

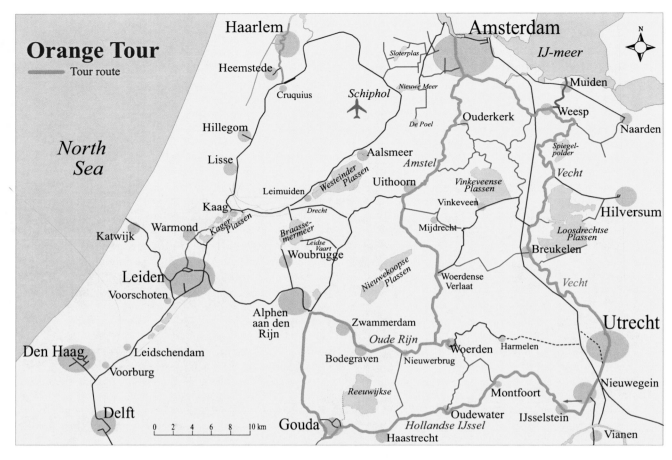

Orange Tour
——— Tour route

North Sea

This loop around the eastern side of the Heart of Holland includes four rivers, the best way to see the countryside of the region. A visit to Amsterdam is optional, depending on the time available; Ouderkerk is the suggested alternate stopover. The days listed below are traveling days; extra days in Utrecht or Amsterdam are by choice.

Day 1 - Begin on the Loosdrechtse Plassen; follow a short connecting channel to the Vecht river. Enjoy most of the day on the Vecht to Utrecht and pass through the city on the Oudegracht, then moor on the Catharinesingel.

Day 2 - Travel on the Hollandse IJssel river, with stops at Montfoort and Oudewater. Arrive at Gouda for an evening visit.

Day 3 - Again visit Gouda in the morning, on to Woerden for an interesting small town visit.

Day 4 - Spend the morning traveling slowly through the peaceful Green Heart; follow the Amstel river into Amsterdam, or stop earlier at Ouderkerk.

Day 5 - Leave Amsterdam via the Amsterdam-Rijnkanaal or travel back through the city on the Amstel. Join the Vecht river at Weesp for a cruise on the northern section of that beautiful river.

Orange Tour: Loosdrechtse Plassen - Utrecht - Gouda - Woerden - Amsterdam - Vecht

WATERWAY Names are as shown on ANWB charts	FROM	TO	KM	LOCKS	BRIDGES to open	DEPTH minimum	WIDTH locks/ bridges	HEIGHT fixed bridges	TRAVEL TIME hours
Drecht (Loosdrecht)	Loosdrechtse Plassen	Vecht river	1.0	1	0	1.6	7.0	none	
Vecht river	Drecht (Loosdrecht)	Utrecht	18.0	1	8	2.1	9.0	4.0	
Oudegracht	Utrecht	Catharinesingel, Utrecht	2.0	0	0	1.4	6.8	3.3	
Day 1		Utrecht	21.0	2	8	1.4	7.0	4.0	3.0
Vaartse Rijn	Utrecht	Amsterdam-Rijnkanaal	3.9	1	4	3.0	6.0	3.3	
Merwede Kanaal	Amsterdam-Rijnkanaal	Doorslag	3.3	1	2	3.1	12.0	none	
Doorslag	Merwede Kanaal	Hollandse IJssel	2.2	1	2	1.7	5.8	4.4	
Hollandse IJssel river	IJsselstein	Oudewater	19.8	0	5	1.7	8.5	4.7	
Hollandse IJssel river	Oudewater	Gouda	12.2	2	5	1.9	6.0	none	
Day 2		Gouda	41.4	5	18	1.4	5.8	3.3	8.5
Nieuwe Gouwe	Gouda	Gouda	1.5	1	2	2.4	9.0	none	
Gouwe	Gouda	Alphen aan den Rijn	14.7	1	6	2.8	14.0	none	
Oude Rijn	Alphen aan den Rijn	Woerden	19.0	1	8	2.5	5.6	none	
Day 3		Woerden	35.2	3	16	2.4	5.6	none	8.5
Oude Rijn	Woerden	Grecht	1.5	0	2	2.2	7.9	none	
Grecht	Oude Rijn	Woerdense Verlaat	8.5	1	1	1.7	5.1	none	
Kromme Mijdrecht	Woerdense Verlaat	Amstel	10.9	0	2	1.9	5.1	none	
Amstel river	Uithoorn (Kromme Mijdrecht)	Weesper Trekvaart	18.0	0	3	2.8	10.5	5.1	
Amstel river	Weesper Trekvaart	Sixhaven Marina	5.1	1	13	2.1	7.7	none	
Day 4		Amsterdam	44.0	2	21	1.7	5.1	5.1	8.0
Amstel river	Het IJ	Weesper Trekvaart	5.1	1	13	2.5	7.7	none	
Weesper Trekvaart	Amstel	Amsterdam-Rijnkanaal	9.0	0	5	2.2	9.0	5.0	
Smal Weesp	Amsterdam-Rijnkanaal	Weesp	1.7	0	4	2.0	8.0	none	
Vecht river	Weesp	Drecht (Loosdrecht)	20.0	0	6	2.1	9.5	none	
Drecht (Loosdrecht)	Vecht river	Loosdrechtse Plassen	1.0	1	0	1.6	7.0	none	
Day 5		Loosdrechtse Plassen	36.8	2	28	1.6	7.0	5.0	8.0
TOTAL			178.4	14	91	1.4	5.1	3.3	36.0

Vecht river

At right is the Roodebrug, at Loevenhoutsedijk in the northern suburbs of Utrecht. Note the bridge watcher's house, very handsome, at the east end of the bridge.

The Vecht, often called the most beautiful river in Europe and certainly the most beautiful in the Netherlands, flows north from Utrecht to the IJsselmeer at Muiden, a total distance of 43 km. It offers a leisure cruise paralleling the Amsterdam-Rijnkanaal, which is a highway for commercial barges.

"Vecht" translates as "Fight". It is possible that the name dates from the time in the Middle Ages when the river was the front line of defense for Amsterdam. It may also derive from the Roman "Fectio", the name of a fort located here. What is definitely true is that the name has nothing at all to do with "fighting" the river. It is a slow, calm stream with no sharp curves. There are no locks along the river, only those at each end (Utrecht and Muiden) and on the sides for access to lakes and canals. In fact the water in the Ijsselmeer is normally higher than that of the Vecht at the lock in Muiden, therefore the flow is reversed and may flow "upstream". Only in the case of very heavy rain will the water flow north to the mouth of the river.

FROM	TO	KM	LOCKS	BRIDGES BB to open	DEPTH minimum	WIDTH locks/ bridges	HEIGHT fixed bridges
Utrecht	Oud-Zuilen	4.9	1	4	2.10	8.10	4.00
Oud-Zuilen	Maarssen	3.7	0	2	2.10	28.00	4.00
Maarssen	Breukelen	5.6	0	2	2.10	8.70	9.60
Breukelen	Nieuwersluis	2.6	0	1	1.80	8.90	none
Nieuwersluis	Loenen	1.7	0	1	2.30	9.60	none
Loenen	Vreeland	3.2	0	3	2.10	9.29	none
Vreeland	Overmeer	2.9	0	0	2.10	none	none
Overmeer	Nigtevecht	4.0	0	0	2.10	none	none
Nigtevecht	Weesp	9.3	0	1	2.40	10.00	none
Weesp	Muiden	5.0	1	5	2.40	7.60	none
		42.9	2	19			

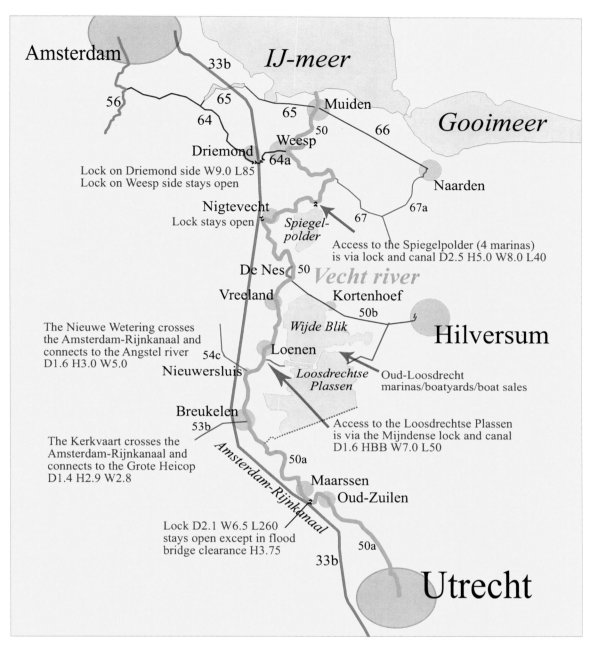

Amsterdam

IJ-meer

33b

Gooimeer

56

65

65   Muiden

64

50

66

Weesp

Driemond   64a

Naarden

Lock on Driemond side W9.0 L85
Lock on Weesp side stays open

67a

Nigtevecht   67

Lock stays open   *Spiegelpolder*

Access to the Spiegelpolder (4 marinas)
is via lock and canal D2.5 H5.0 W8.0 L40

De Nes   50   *Vecht river*

Vreeland   Kortenhoef

Wijde Blik   50b

Hilversum

The Nieuwe Wetering crosses
the Amsterdam-Rijnkanaal and
connects to the Angstel river
D1.6 H3.0 W5.0   54c

Loenen

Nieuwersluis   *Loosdrechtse
Plassen*   Oud-Loosdrecht
marinas/boatyards/boat sales

Breukelen

53b

Access to the Loosdrechtse Plassen
is via the Mijndense lock and canal
D1.6 HBB W7.0 L50

The Kerkvaart crosses the
Amsterdam-Rijnkanaal and
connects to the Grote Heicop
D1.4 H2.9 W2.8

Amsterdam-Rijnkanaal

50a

Maarssen

Oud-Zuilen

Lock D2.1 W6.5 L260
stays open except in flood
bridge clearance H3.75

50a

33b

Utrecht

Waterways shown on this map are:

33b Amsterdam-Rijnkanaal	50,50a Vecht river
50b Hilversum Kanaal	53b Grote Heicop
54c Angstel river	56 Amstel river
64 Weesper Trekvaart	64a Smal Weesp
65 Muidertrekvaart	66 Naardertrekvaart
67 's-Gravelandse Vaart	67a Karnemelk-sloot

Utrecht

Utrecht is a beautiful city that is smaller and more easily viewed than Amsterdam on foot or bike, without the huge crowds. This university town offers many restaurants, cafes and terraces lining the Oudegracht as it passes directly through the center of the city. The old wharves and vaulted cellars are under the shops and residences that line the streets one story above the canal.

 A full day or much more can be spent here, shopping, dining and visiting the many sights; these include two historic churches, the Dom and the Janskerhof, as well as museums and old houses, along with significant modern architectural buildings and homes.

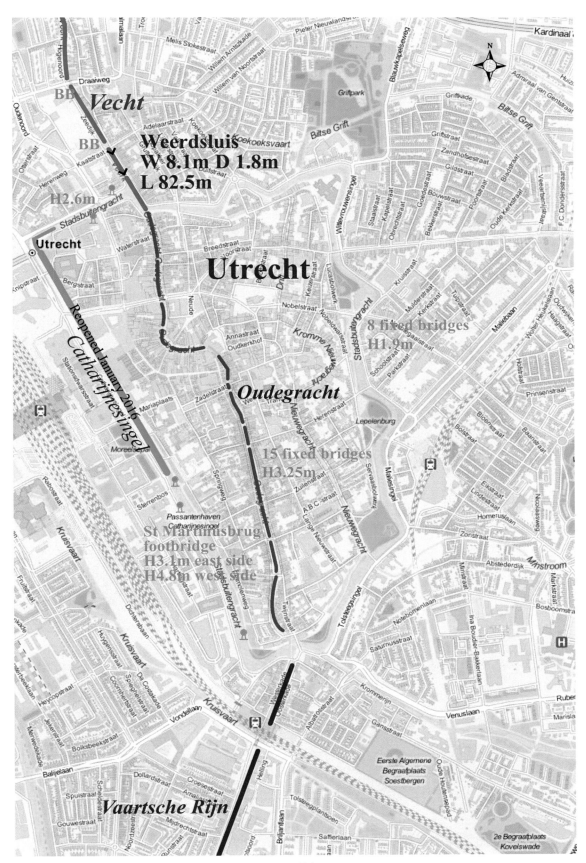

Vecht

BB

BB

Weerdsluis
W 8.1m D 1.8m
L 82.5m

H2.6m

Stadsbuitengracht

Utrecht

Utrecht

Reopened January 2016

Catharijnesingel

Oudegracht

8 fixed bridges
H1.9m

15 fixed bridges
H3.25m

St Martinusbrug
footbridge
H3.1m east side
H4.8m west side

Vaartsche Rijn

Oud-Zuilen

A small, beautiful village offering moorings on the west bank of the river, a well-known restaurant, Bistro Belle, and 't Slot castle/museum. The most famous resident of the castle was Belle van Zuylen (Isabelle de Charrière), well-known writer and feminist, and namesake for the restaurant.
www.bistrobelle.nl
www.slotzuylen.nl

Maarssen

There are plentiful moorings along the river bank with shops and restaurants, as well as restored homes and manor houses.

The 100meter-long connection into the Amsterdam-Rijnkanaal is at the south end of Maarssen (viewed from Amsterdam-Rijnkanaal.)
The lock stays open except in flood; bridge clearance is 3.75m.
This lock is useful for boaters wanting to travel the Vecht but avoid the city of Utrecht.

Breukelen

The namesake for Brooklyn USA is a popular place for restaurants, shops and gawking at the beautiful homes and manor houses along the river. Moorings are available along the west bank at the north of town.

Breukelen is sandwiched between the Vecht and the Amsterdam-Rijnkanaal; the Kerkvaart Danne connects west across the middle of town to the Amsterdam-Rijnkanaal and on westward to the Vinkeveense Plassen. The 0.7km-long (and very narrow) Dannegracht/Kerkvaart offers small boats a route to the Vinkeveense and Nieuwkoopse lakes; the recommended draft is 0.7m, height 2.9m and width is 2.8m.

The Vecht is a waterway of style, intricate and twisty. Atmospheric mansions line its banks,with numerous summerhouses among the willow trees and an elegant castle at Nijenrode, upstream of Breukelen...
John Liley, "Barge Country"

53

Loenen

The northbound approach to Loenen is one of the most striking on the Vecht river; the tower of the medieval church, the classic split-span bridge and the beautiful houses with flowerbeds along the waterfront draw boaters for a visit. However, the moorings are south of the town, on the west bank, where the town provides a grass riverbank mooring. It's a short walk into town but one block off the river, so you may want to come in for this view and then turn back to tie up.

There are more than the usual number of fine restaurants in these towns along the Vecht, especially in Loenen, probably a result of the pleasant views and the easy access from larger cities. This is a popular region, and not just for boaters. Some of these are elegant and expensive but there is a wide range of choices, from pizza and pasta to fine dining. In Loenen you can choose from Tante Koosje, De Proeverij, Brasserie Het Amsterdammertje and De Eterij, along with others.

The mooring at Loenen is a good place for a 5km bicycle ride: cross the bridge south of the mooring then cycle north on a narrow lane. Enjoy the view of the elegant homes on the east side of the river and the woonboten permanently moored on both sides of the river between Loenen and Vreeland. The turnaround point is in the center of Vreeland, where a suggested stop for coffee and pastry is at Bakkerij P. Boonzaaijer on the east bank north of the Breedstraat bridge.

Loosdrechtse Plassen

The five Loosdrecht lakes are interconnected, creating a beautiful water sports area. All types of vessels are permitted; along with the many motorboats which use these waters, you can rent a canoe, rowboat, sailboat or sloep. In the lakes are islands with beautiful beaches, ideal for a picnic. Or tie up your boat at one of the cozy restaurants on the waterfront.   www.vvvwijdemeren.nl

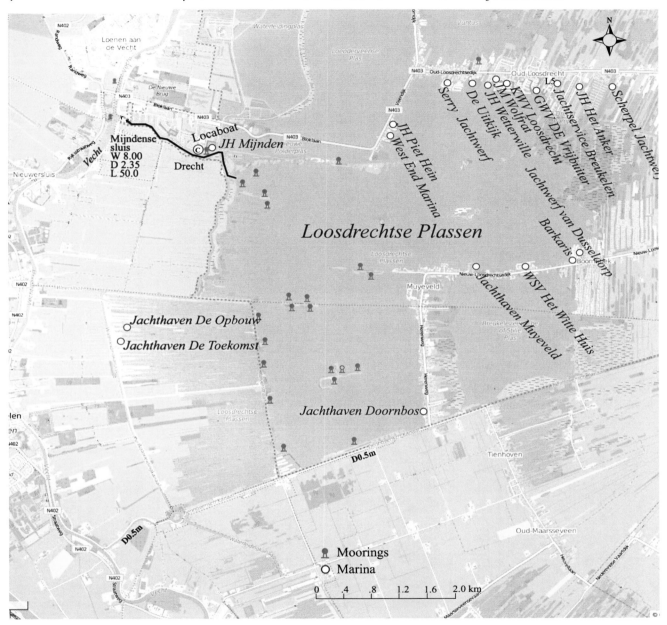

The canal east from the Vecht into Loosdrechtse Plassen is less than a kilometer south of the village of Loenen, through the lock Mijndensesluis (maximum draft 1.2m.) The lock itself is unusual, in that it is a 50m-long curve, a tight one; from the west gate you cannot see the east gate because of the curve. Along the canal are the rental-boat base of Locaboat and Jachthaven Mijnden. There are many boat clubs, jachthaven and boat brokers in the northeastern corner of the lake, at Oud Loosdrecht. Note that the lake is shallow and attention to the chart is important.

Vreeland

Best waterfront village: Vreeland, on the Vecht river, offers a visitor's quay right in the center of the town. Throughout the river's length through the town, flowers and shrubs of residents' yards run right over the banks of the river. Their own small boats are moored at almost every house, the various styles and shapes adding to the interest of the view. The graceful, symmetrical white structures of the lifting bridge in the middle of town make a beautiful sight next to the handsome white bridgekeeper's house. This is definitely a town where travelers should cruise very slowly and then tie-up on the grassy bank for a walk along the narrow brick streets past the charming homes, and a visit to the bakery.

Hilversums Kanaal

At De Nes, the bend in the Vecht that resembles a nose, the Hiversum canal branches to the east through the Hemeltje lock. Commercial traffic is bound for the city of Hilversum, 8 km east. Pleasure boaters may want to go as far as the windmill Gabriel (1 km, at the far distance in the photo at right below) or to a mooring in the Wijde Blik lake (1.5 km.) The ancient Fort Kijkuit is nearby on the canal bank next to the windmill.

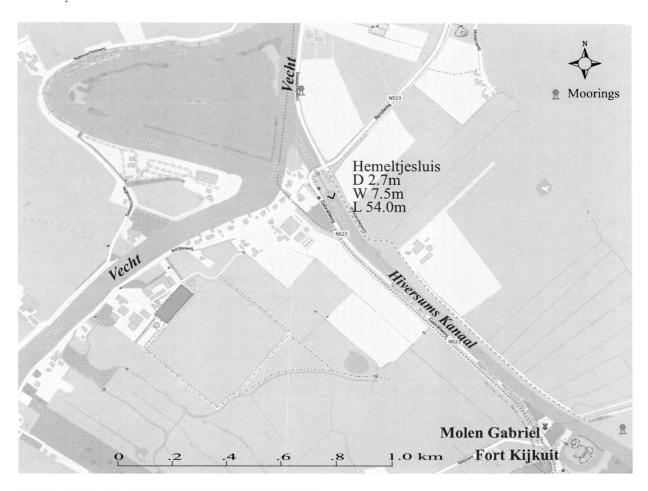

Weesp

Weesp has its own Oudegracht, through the center of town as does Utrecht. The gracht here is not navigable, it is filled with beautiful water lilies. In the summer baskets and urns of flowers along the park strips overflow with purple and white pansies.

WV de Zeemeermin
de-zeemeermin-weesp.nl
0294 431 588

WV Weesp   wv-weesp.nl   0638 397 883

WSV de Vecht   wsvdevecht.nl   0294 412 700

The town has a protected historical center with many buildings dating from the seventeenth and eighteenth century, along with two windmills, De Eendragt and De Vriendschap, on the west bank of the Vecht just south of town (and just before arriving at WSV De Vecht.)

Muiden

Muiden, located at the mouth of the Vecht on the IJmeer, is a boater's town. The river passes through a lock and a lifting bridge right in the middle of town; yacht brokers, boatyards and marinas are located on the sea-side of the lock. Cafe tables on the lock wall are popular for watching the dozens of boats passing through on summer weekends.

The rental boat shown above is tied-up on the west bank of the Vecht; behind it are the bunkers of Fortress Muiden and straight across is the Muiderslot castle, a restored 13th-century moated castle with ramparts & a hands-on museum, plus formal gardens.
www.muiderslot.nl

Jachthaven Fort H jachthavenforth.nl
0294 433 154
Jachthaven Stichting Muiden
jachthavenmuiden.nl 0294 26 12 23

Hollandse IJssel river

The Hollandse IJssel between Nieuwegein and Gouda is a popular cross-country route. It has little commercial barge traffic along its winding rural path and the riverside sights are very pleasant. There is one lock, just above Gouda and three towns which offer good services for overnight stops.

IJsselstein

There are many shops on the pedestrianized streets, with bus service into Utrecht. Moorings are on a long quay. Marnemonde Marina, restaurant and Delos yacht charter base is 3kms west, in the countryside.

www.marnemoende.nl

030 60 60 663

Montfoort

There is little of historical interest but a pleasant small town for a quiet stop with shops and restaurants. You can visit and dine at the Kasteel Montfoort.   www.kasteel-montfoort.nl

Hollandse IJssel river

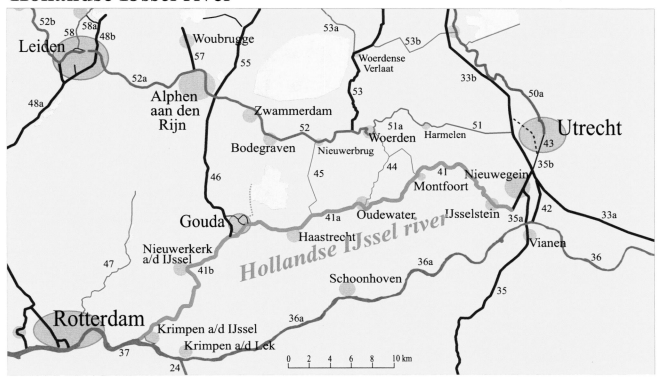

Hollandse IJssel river is an ancient branch (now closed) of the Lek; both are part of the Rhine delta.
It flows past Gouda to the Lek/Nieuwe Maas, which continues west past Rotterdam to the North Sea.
The Nieuwe Maas can be used to connect with canals north to Delft, however the river is very busy
with barge traffic and can have strong current; recommended only for experienced skippers.

WATERWAY	FROM	TO	KM	LOCKS	BRIDGES to open	DEPTH minimum	WIDTH locks/ bridges	HEIGHT fixed bridges
Vaartse Rijn	Utrecht	Amsterdam-Rijnkanaal	3.9	1	4	3.0	6.0	3.3
Merwede Kanaal	Amsterdam-Rijnkanaal	Nieuwegein	2.1	1	2	3.1	12.0	none
Doorslag	Nieuwegein	IJsselstein	2.2	1	2	1.7	5.8	4.4
Hollandse IJssel	IJsselstein	Montfoort	12.4	0	3	1.7	12.0	4.7
Hollandse IJssel	Montfoort	Oudewater	7.4	0	2	1.5/1.0	8.5	none
Hollandse IJssel	Oudewater	Haastrecht	7.5	0	2	1.9	7.5	none
Hollandse IJssel	Haastrecht	Gouda	4.7	1	3	1.9	6.0	none
Hollandse IJssel	Gouda	Nieuwe Maas river	16.6	0	0	3.0	n/a	none
			56.8					

HAVENS - Hollandse IJssel river

Town	Type	Name	Telephone	Website	Email
Gouda	boat club	WV Gouda	0614 884 345	www.watersportvereniging-gouda nl	n/a
Gouda	marina	Gemeente Gouda	0182 516 019	www.gouda.nl	n/a
Montfoort	marina	Gemeente Montfoor	0348 47 64 00	www.montfoort.nl	n/a
IJsselstein	marina	Jachthaven Marnemoende	0306 060 663	www.marnemoende.nl	n/a
IJsselstein	marina	Gemeente IJsselstei	14 030	www.ijsselstein.nl	n/a
Nieuwegein	marina	Hatenboer Jachtverhuur	0306 032 773	www.hatenboer.nl	Niels.van.Duuren@gmail.com

Oudewater

Known for the "witches scale" where women were weighed; those judged too heavy to ride a broomstick were deemed to not be a witch. Heksenwaag museum tells this story; the nearby Touwmuseum displays the town's history in making rope from locally-grown hemp. visit-oudewater.nl/en/
There are plentiful riverside moorings through the town.
www.oudewater.nl
14-0348

For a view of the town and surroundings, climb the tower of St Michaëlskerk (below.)
Walk the banks of the Lange Linschoten river (above) as it curves through the town.

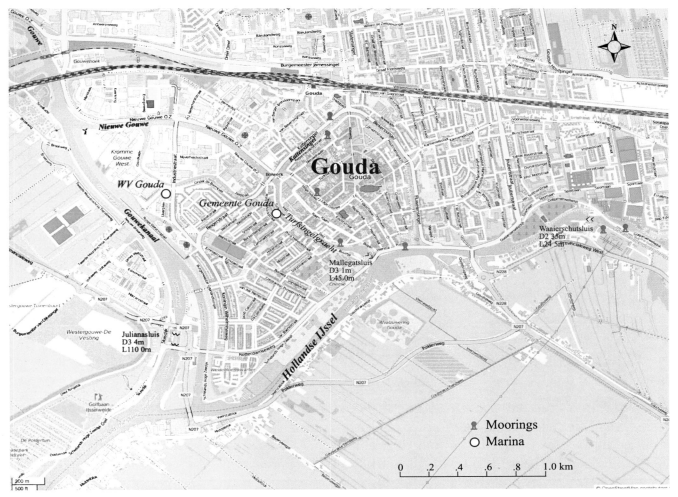

Gouda is a city of canals; vessels are permitted on most. Fixed bridges are few, except for the small-boat route northeast to Reeuwijkse. The Hollandse IJssel continues on southwest to the major city of Rotterdam or south to Dordrecht. Vessels arriving from the east can enter the canals of the city through Mallegatsluis and pass by the historic sailing barges at the haven museum; continue on for moorings on the canals which surround the inner city of Gouda.   www.museumhavengouda.nl

A short walk from a mooring along the quays right in the middle of the city, visitors can select from cheeses or handicrafts at markets held in the main square. Located at this square are the beautiful 15th century Gothic *Stadhuis* (city hall, see photo) and the magnificent collection of 70 stained glass windows in St.-Janskerk, along with more than a dozen outdoor cafes. The Gouda Cheese Market is a spectacular and historic scene, held every Thursday morning. www.welkomingouda.nl/en

(See photos of arrival from the north on page 96.)

Oude Rijn river

The Oude Rijn (Old Rhine) west from Woerden is a pleasant cruise. The river curves slowly through the agricultural heart of Holland, from Utrecht to Leiden, and on to the sea at Katwijk. Scattered homes line the riverbanks, most of them with gardens. The occasional group of industrial buildings seem out of place here, but they are unobtrusive and quickly left behind. It is perfect for a slow cruise.

Nieuwerbrug is a quiet, charming small village, strung along the banks of the Oude Rijn.

Oude Rijn river

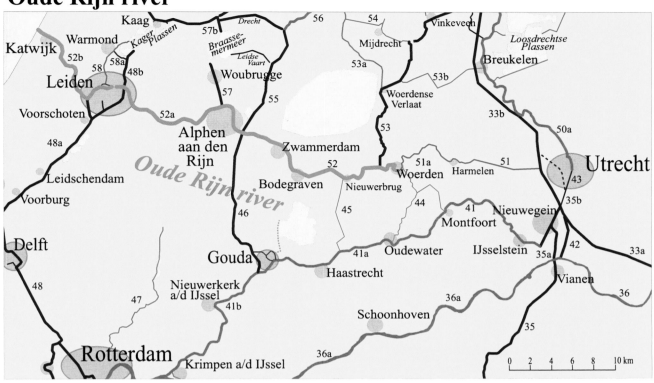

The Oude Rijn river is a major east-west route, with significant towns to visit, as well as connecting across north-south routes. The Leidse Rijn/Oude Rijn river from Utrecht to Woerden is not navigable by cruising boats, as there are low fixed bridges. The river continues west from Leiden into the North Sea, however there is no navigable outlet to the sea.

FROM	TO	KM	LOCKS	BRIDGES to open	DEPTH minimum	WIDTH locks/ bridges	HEIGHT fixed bridges
Woerden (Grecht)	Nieuwerbrug	5.6	0	3	2.2	5.7	none
Nieuwerbrug	Bodegraven	5.0	1	1	2.2	5.6	none
Bodegraven	Zwammerdam	2.8	0	2	2.5	10.5	none
Zwammerdam	Aarkanaal	4.1	0	1	2.5	12.0	none
Aarkanaal	Alphen@Heimanswetering	3.8	0	4	2.8	4.4	none
Alphen	Leiderdorp@Does	9.3	0	1	2.5	10.0	none
Leiderdorp	Leiden (passantenhaven)	3.4	0	4	2.5	10.5	none
Woerden (Grecht)	Leiden (passantenhaven)	34.0	1	16			

HAVENS - Oude Rijn river

Town	Type	Name	Telephone	Website	Email
Woerden	boat club	WSV De Greft	0348 411 909	www.degreft.nl	secretaris@degreft.nl
Woerden	marina	Binnenstadhaven Woerden	06 31 95 73 11	www.degreft.nl	n/a
Alphen a/d Rijn	marina	Haven aan den Rijn	06 36 36 74 28	www.havenaandenrijn.nl	n/a
Alphen a/d Rijn	boat club	WV Alphen a/d Rijn	0172 435 090	wvalphen.nl	n/a
Alphen a/d Rijn	marina	Gemeente Alphen a/d Rijn	0172 430 955	www.alphenaandenrijn.nl	n/a
Leiderdorp	boat club	WV Doeshaven	06 26 84 91 12	www.doeshaven.nl	info@doeshaven.nl

Woerden

There is history to be seen in Woerden. The tourist office (VVV) offers a list of 49 national monuments within the town, including Woerden Castle. The castle is a very impressive block of brick, with low cylindrical towers on each of the four corners; it was built in 1404. It originally was surrounded by a moat but in these modern days two arms of the moat have been filled-in and paved for a parking lot.

The Oude Rijn river passes through the town on the singel (moat) of the star fort. This star fort is not as spectacular as that at Naarden, as no fortifications remain and the shape is only clear in an aerial view. However it does remain as a moat around the town which makes for very pleasant walking or biking.

Unusually not located directly on the water, the windmill De Windhond is set atop an earthen mound, thus it towers over the southwestern part of the town.

Bodegraven

Almost every town in the Netherlands has a boating club; these berths (above) in Bodegraven are reserved for the members of WV De Oude Rijn. There are moorings for visitors at a quay on the south bank in the town center.

Alphen aan den Rijn

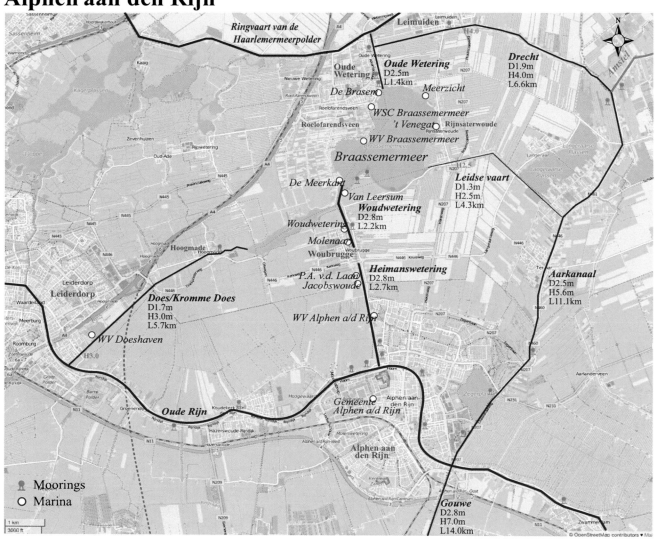

This small city spreads out on both sides of the Oude Rijn west of the Aarkanaal intersection; it is an important intersection of the waterways between Woerden and Leiden. The waterway coming up from the south (at Gouda) is the Gouwe, a canalized river; north of the Oude Rijn it becomes the Aarkanaal, headed toward the Amstel river and Amsterdam. The canals Heimanswetering and Woudwetering lead to Woubrugge and the Braassemermeer.

The route north from Gouda passes through Boskoop. There are three hefbrug on this canal; on this type of bridge the entire span travels straight up, lifted by cables on tall towers, one on each bank; the canal is relatively wide and even a span hinged at both ends would be too long to lift. The cable towers are steel-girder construction, resembling an oil drilling rig, and are a strange sight in this otherwise horizontal landscape. The result is ugly and rather jarring.

Leiden

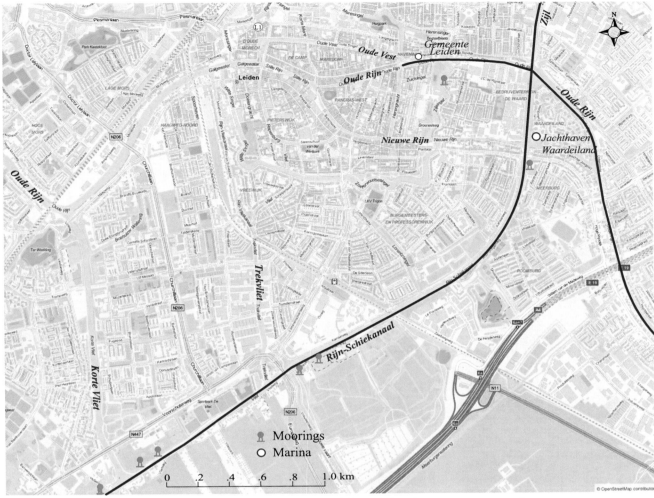

Leiden is a city of canals, floating cafes and many bridges. That's easy to say, as there are many towns and cities in Holland with the same description. But there are more here than in most, perhaps second only to Amsterdam, a much larger city; there are two dozen named canals and 88 bridges inside the singel ring.

Most of the canals are lined by small boats and houseboats, too many to count. The boats have to be small, as many of the bridges are low and do not open. Those on the Oude Rijn, which passes west from the city docks, as well as those on the Oude Vest across the center of the city, are 1.3 meters clearance. To travel on to a jachthaven at Katwijk (no access through to the North Sea) take the canals around the south of Leiden: Rijn-Schiekanaal & Korte Vliet.

Mijdrecht - Woerdense Verlaat - Nieuwkoop

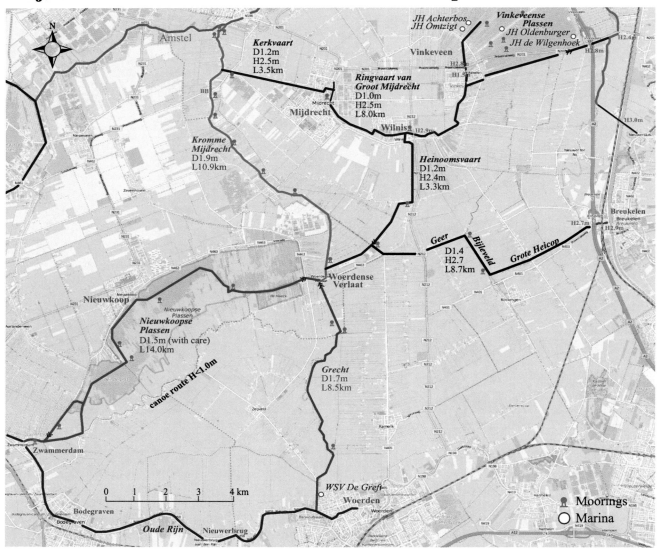

This region is truly the "Green Heart" of the Netherlands. The flora in the waters and along the banks stretch off into the distance, a sea of greenery. Boaters can view and hear the calls of many water and grassland birds. Isolated moorings are plentiful, away from city sounds and lights.

Woerdense Verlaat is a good destination in this area; it's easy to find a quiet mooring but there is a cafe/restaurant in the town as well as Slikkendam Watersport boat services. www.slikkendam.nl

Nieuwkoopse Plassen is a natural area of 1400 hectares; of this, more than 1000 hectares have been preserved by the Natuurmonumenten. The lakes remain from the removal of peat in the 16th century. This area is ideal for exploration by canoe or kayak, however larger boats must navigate with care.

The Geer Bijleveld and Grote Heicop combine to offer a route (with restrictive dimensions) leading east to the Vecht river at Breukelen.

Amstel River

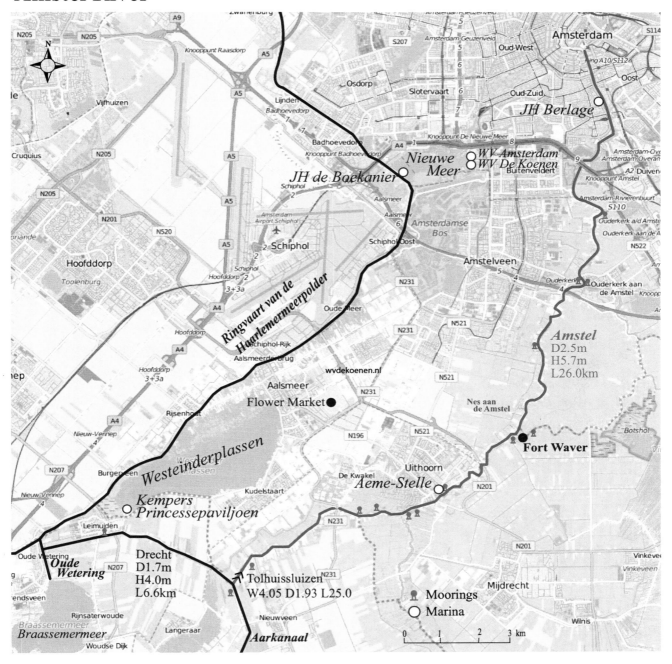

The Amstel follows a curving path as it flows north into the center of Amsterdam, where it ends in a series of the city's canals. On both sides of the elevated waterway the land drops away quickly to the level of the fields about five meters below. The fields are dotted with herds of dairy cows. As you travel you can look across the absolutely flat fields and see the spires of churches above the clumps of trees that mark small villages.

Although the Amstel is not far away from the popular Westeinderplassen, there are no direct waterway connections. Access is only from the Ringvaart van de Harlemermeerpolder.

Jachthaven Aeme-Stelle   www.aeme-stelle.nl   06 48 45 46 63

71

uderkerk - Vinkeveense Plassen

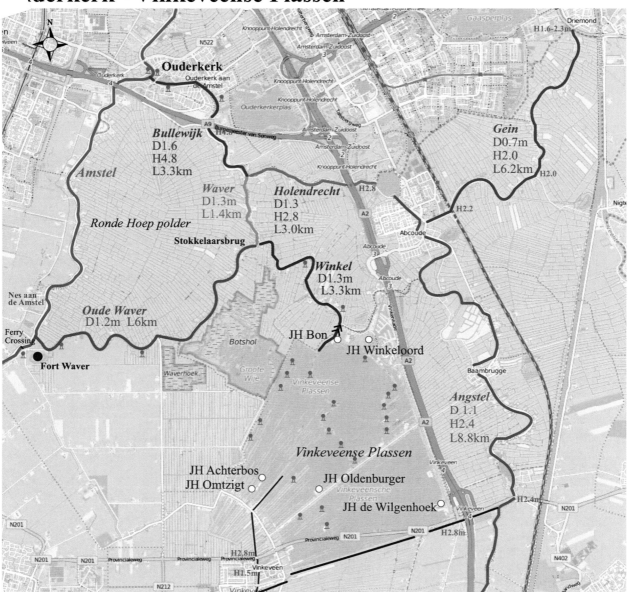

Ouderkerk aan de Amstel: This is a charming, peaceful village with riverbank moorings on the Amstel and the Bullewijk. Terraces on the river offer open-air dining, with dining rooms across the roadway. Here or at moorings on the Amstel for the next 3km north would be a good overnight stop for a visit to Amsterdam; the Amsterdam Metro line to Amstelveen is less than 2 km west of the Amstel moorings.   www.amsterdam.info/transport/metro/

Vinkeveense Plassen: These are excellent waterways on which to explore and enjoy the Heart of Holland. Small boats are recommended. Note the restrictive dimensions shown on this map; Depth and Height shown are the minimum for that waterway. The Waver and Oude Waver are open as to height, entirely served by BB bridges. East of the Autoroute A2 is a very attractive area, but with more restrictive depth and height; plan carefully. Perhaps rent a sloep at JH Winkeloord for the six hour loop along the Angstel and Holendrecht; Baambrugge is a special town to visit.

Amsterdam-Rijnkanaal

This straight, wide canal is a highway for commercial barges, although it can be used by pleasure boats as well. There are three connections between the Vecht river and the Amsterdam-Rijnkanaal: at Weesp, Nigtevecht and Maarssen. These locks normally stay open and are closed only at times of flood. Small boats can pass from the Vecht under the Amsterdam-Rijnkanaal at Nieuwersluis or Breukelen to travel into the smaller waterways and lakes of the Heart of Holland. Above, a fully loaded sand barge passes under the Weesperbrug.

Below: crossing the canal between Driemond and Weesp; the recommended procedure is to turn to your right, with traffic, for 100 meters before turning across. Thus you will make a U-crossing, rather than straight across through two-way traffic.

Weesper Trekvaart entrance at Driemond, on the west bank.

Smal Weesp entrance, on the east bank.

AMSTERDAM

The largest, and most well-known, city in the Netherlands is Amsterdam, named for the dam on the Amstel. The river leads from the beautiful Heart of Holland countryside directly into the center of the city. Traveling north on the river, the first notice of the city ahead are the tall office towers, then the boxy apartment buildings of the suburbs. Then you quickly arrive among the narrow four- and five-story rowhouses which line the streets and canals.

Six primary canals are semicircular concentric rings, centered on the point where the Amstel joins the east-west river IJ. These are connected at various points by short canals, and crossed by the radial streets. It is a city that favored pedestrian and cycle traffic as it grew; those continue to be the popular means of transport, along with the water taxis and tour boats which travel the canals day and night. There are literally thousands of vessels tied up along the banks of every canal, from dinghies used to dart about as personal transport, old tugboats and workboats, steel cruisers built since WWII, to active or retired barges and immovable houseboats.

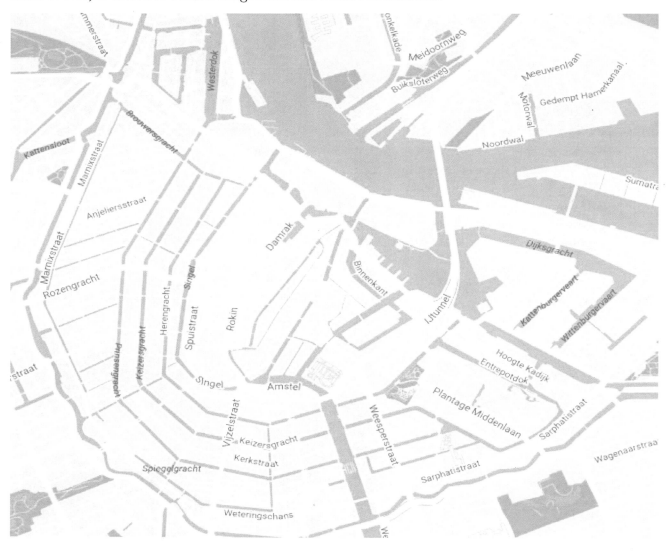

Cruising into Amsterdam

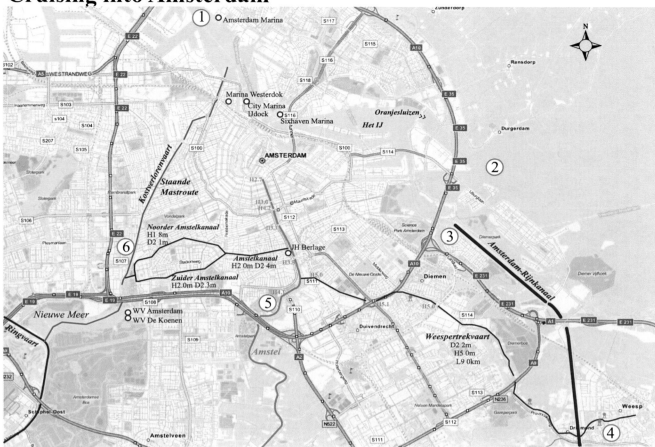

It is possible to cruise the canals inside the city of Amsterdam on your own boat; you can choose from six approach routes. The first three offer essentially unrestricted bridge clearance, while the latter three, which are the focus of this guide, restrict the height of your boat.

1) Nordzeekanaal - From the North Sea, Noord Holland canals or the Haarlem area.

2) IJmeer/Het IJ - From the mouth of the Vecht river at Muiden, across the open water of the IJmeer and into Het Ij via the lock complex Oranjesluizen.

3) Amsterdam-Rijnkanaal - Leads into Het IJ with no locks but with heavy barge traffic.

4) Weesper Trekvaart - From the Vecht river at Weesp or the Amsterdam-Rijnkanaal to Amstel.
   6 fixed bridges Height 5.0m Depth 2.4m

5) Amstel river - From the center of the Heart of Holland waterways into the center of Amsterdam.
   5 fixed bridges Height 3.0m Depth 3.3m

6) Ringvaart/Nieuwe Meer - From Ringvaart Van De Haarlemmermeerpolder & Nieuwe Meer
   and then two choices: a) Kostverlorenvaart & Kattensloot to Het IJ
   9 BB bridges Height (when closed) 2.5m Depth 2.0m
   b) Olympia channel & Zuider Amstelkanaal to Amstel river
   14 fixed bridges Height 2.0m Depth 2.3m

SIXHAVEN MARINA

To visit Amsterdam the best mooring option is "Sixhaven". There is a free ferry (24/7) to Centraal rail station (the long building in the photo above.) From there you can walk in about 10 minutes to the center of Amsterdam. Mooring costs in Sixhaven (2017): 9 meter boat €15,30, 15 m €30,60/night. www.sixhaven.nl 0206 32 94 29 (Reservations not accepted.)

An alternate is Amsterdam Marina, located on Het IJ 2.6 km west of Sixhaven. €2,50/meter/night. www.amsterdammarina.com 0206 31 07 67

Sixhaven Marina is on Het IJ, so when departing your stay it is a short route east to the IJsselmeer. But to stay on the inland waterways, use the Amstel river, southbound. To leave Sixhaven for the Amstel cross through the busy traffic on Het IJ to Oosterdok. Stay clear of barges and ferry boats full of commuters. (See map on next page.) On the south side of the river pass under two BB bridges (H5.1m), then the Oosterdokdraaibrug (H2.85m) to enter Marine Haven. This is a possible mast-up route between the IJ and the Amstel, however there are 5.0m fixed bridges on the south of the city.

Nieuwe Herengracht leads into the center of Amsterdam past six BB bridges (H2.40m) and one lock, normally open; then go south across the center of the canal ring on the Amstel river. The bridges on the Amstel are high enough and the Amstelsluis is usually open, so boats can cruise comfortably up the river, leaving the city southbound on the Amstel or turning east at the edge of the city onto the Weesper Trekvaart, to Weesp and the Vecht or the Amsterdam/Rijnkanaal.

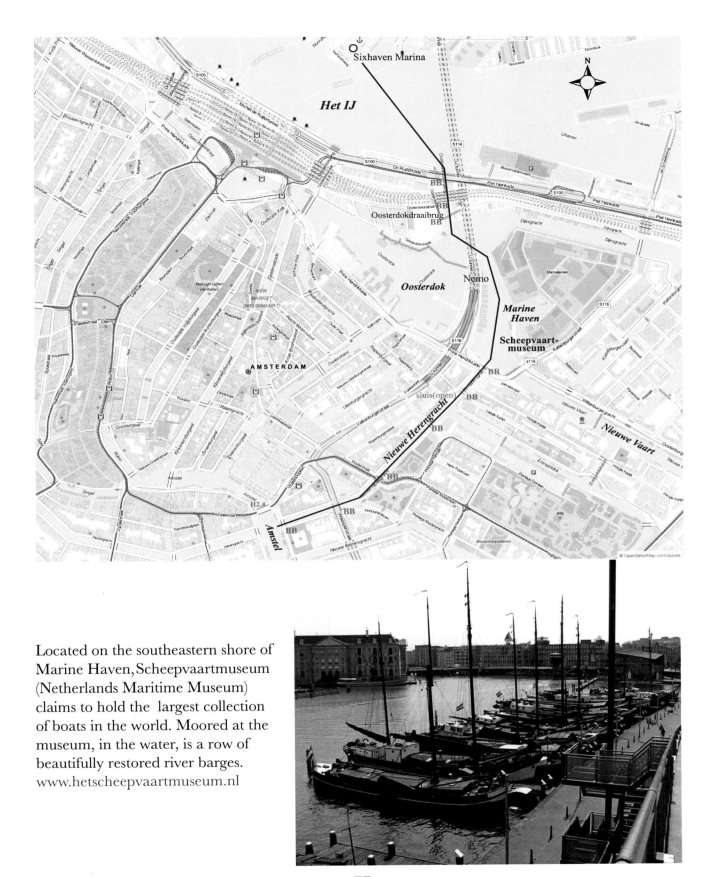

Located on the southeastern shore of
Marine Haven, Scheepvaartmuseum
(Netherlands Maritime Museum)
claims to hold the largest collection
of boats in the world. Moored at the
museum, in the water, is a row of
beautifully restored river barges.
www.hetscheepvaartmuseum.nl

77

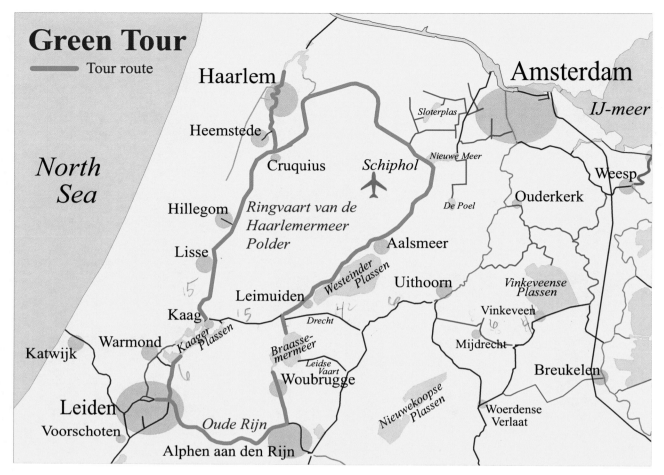

Green Tour

— Tour route

Haarlem

Amsterdam

IJ-meer

Heemstede

Sloterplas

North Sea

Cruquius

Schiphol

Nieuwe Meer

Weesp

Hillegom

Ringvaart van de Haarlemermeer Polder

De Poel

Ouderkerk

Lisse

Aalsmeer

Westeinder Plassen

Uithoorn

Vinkeveense Plassen

Leimuiden

Vinkeveen

Kaag

Drecht

Kaager Plassen

Braasse-mermeer

Mijdrecht

Warmond

Katwijk

Leidse Vaart

Woubrugge

Nieuwekoopse Plassen

Breukelen

Leiden

Woerdense Verlaat

Voorschoten

Oude Rijn

Alphen aan den Rijn

The northwestern corner of the Heart of Holland is explored in this tour, which can be completed in as little as two days. But then the travelers would miss out on sightseeing in two of Holland's most interesting cities, Haarlem and Leiden, and enjoying the waters of some very pleasant lakes.

Day 1 - Leave Kaager Plassen and begin a clockwise circuit of Ringvaart van de Haarlemermeer Polder. In March through May, moor in Lisse for a visit to the world famous Keukenhof Gardens. At Cruiquis turn north onto the Spaarne river, to a quayside mooring in the center of Haarlem.

Day 2 - Return to the Ringvaart and steer toward Amsterdam; if time allows, visit the city via the Nieuwe Meer. Otherwise continue around the Ringvaart and enter Westeinder Plassen, mooring at Aalsmeer or near Leimuiden.

Day 3 - Exit the lake on the south via Woubrugge and follow the Oude Rijn river to the city of Leiden.

Day 4 - Spend the day touring Leiden or at the beach of Katwijk; the Oude Rijn empties at the coast, however there is no through-passage channel for boats. Tie up less than 1km from the beach for an afternoon or overnight visit. Low bridges through Leiden mean that you must get there on canals around the east and south of the city before rejoining the Oude Rijn.

Day 5 - Leave Leiden on the Zijl and explore the southern islands and beaches of Kaager Plassen.

Green tour: Kaag - Haarlem - Aalsmeer - Braassemermeer - Leiden - Kaager Plassen

WATERWAY Names are as shown on ANWB charts	FROM	TO	KM	LOCKS	BRIDGES to open	DEPTH minimum	WIDTH locks/ bridges	HEIGHT fixed bridges	TRAVEL TIME hours
Ringvaart van de Haarlemmeerpolder	Kaager Plassen	Cruiquis	16.0	0	9	2.5	7.9	none	
Spaarne river	Cruiquis	Haarlem	6.5	0	9	2.5	8.5	none	
Day 1		Haarlem	22.5		18		7.9	none	5.0
Spaarne river	Haarlem	Cruiquis	6.5	0	9	2.5	8.5	none	
Ringvaart van de Haarlemmeerpolder	Cruiquis	Westeinder Plassen	32.8	0	4	2.5	8.0	5.3	
Day 2		Aalsmeer	39.3	0	13	2.5	8.0	5.3	6.0
Ringvaart van de Haarlemmeerpolder	Westeinder Plassen	Weteringbrug	4.8	0	1	2.5	14.0	none	
Oude Wetering	Ringvaart	Braassemermeer	1.4	0	0	2.5	36.0	none	
Day 5		Braassemermeer	4.8	0	1	2.5	14.0	none	1.0
Woudwetering	Braassemermeer	Alphen aan den Rijn	4.8	0	2	2.8	14.0	none	
Oude Rijn	Alphen aan den Rijn	Leiden (passantenhaven)	12.5	0	5	2.5	10.0	none	
Day 2		Leiden	17.3	0	7	2.5	14.0	none	3.0
Zijl	Leiden	Kaager Plassen	5.6	0	4	2.8	10.5	none	
Kaager Plassen	Zijl	Kaag	3.2	0	0	1.0	open	none	
Day 7		Kaag	8.8	0	3	2.4	10.4	none	1.0
TOTAL			92.7	0	42	1.0	7.9	5.3	16.0

Ringvaart van de Haarlemmermeerpolder

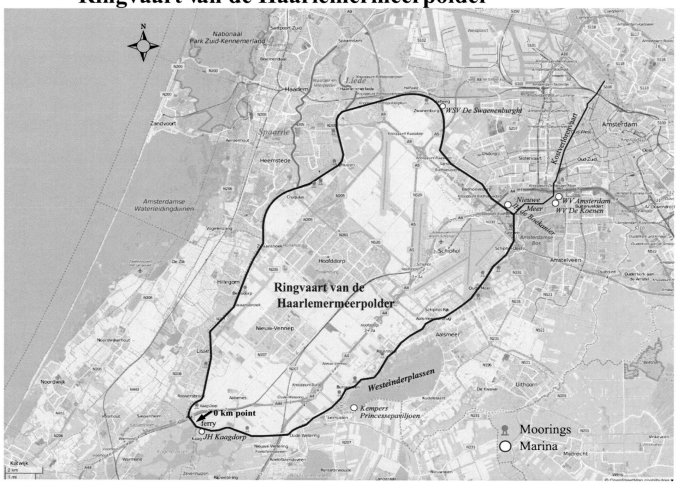

ANWB chart shows distance from Kaag, clockwise.

TOWN	KM	LOCKS	BRIDGES to open	DEPTH minimum	WIDTH locks/ bridges	HEIGHT fixed bridges
Kaag	0.0	0	3	2.3	7.9	none
Lisse	4.5	0	2	2.5	8.1	none
Hillegom	8.5	0	2	2.5	8.1	none
Cruquis	16.0	0	2	2.5	8.5	none
Buiten Liede river	21.8	0	1	2.5	8.0	5.3
Halfweg	27.0	0	1	2.6	8.4	5.6
Slotervaart	33.0	0	1	2.5	8.5	5.8
Nieuwe Meer	35.4	0	1	2.4	16.0	none
Wijde Gat	48.8	0	2	2.5	13.7	none
Leimuiderbrug	51.2	0	2	2.4	10.5	none
Ade river	56.6	0	1	2.5	11.0	none
Kaag	60.0	0	0	2.5	none	none

Staande Mastroute Note: (see page 23) All bridges on the Ringvaart are BB opening bridges EXCEPT the fixed bridges at five locations on the northern section, between Cruquius and Nieuwe Meer, where the lowest clearance is 5.3m. Thus the usual route for taller boats is along the eastern leg of Ringvaart and through the Nieuwe Meer to Kostverlorenvaart. A west-side alternative is the Spaarne river at Haarlem; all bridges there are BB. Some bridges open on a restricted schedule.

Ringvaart van de Haarlemermeerpolder

The name is a mouthful, usually shortened simply to "Ringvaart".
It translates as "Ring for sailing around the Harlem lake polder".

But what is a polder? In the 14th & 15th centuries windmills came into use to pump water from low-lying lands, creating the first polders. Polders are defined as land reclaimed from the sea, a lake or marshland. Some polders are above sea level and surplus water is returned to the sea through locks. When the polder lies below sea level, as many do, the water must be pumped into canals. This is now accomplished by a combination of traditional windmills, modern windmills and diesel or electric motor-driven pumps. The Haarlemmermeerpolder became dry land in 1852.

The Haarlemmermeer polder includes the land under and around Schiphol airport. The canal and dike system that rings this polder encloses over 178 sq km, at a level that averages 4m lower than the sea. This canal connects the Kaager Plassen, Westeinder Plassen and Brassemermeer with the cities of Haarlem, Aalsmeer, Leiden and Alphen, as well as a direct route into the west side of Amsterdam.

The Ringvaart is a man-made canal, for most of its length with straight banks at a uniform width. It feels like traveling on an autoroute, with occasional exits and interchanges. There are, however, boats locally moored along the banks of the canal.

Kaager Plassen

The Kaag lakes are the last parts of historical landscape between Amsterdam and Leiden, not reclaimed from the sea as most of the area has been. The name means "Land outside the dikes." Kaag, a picturesque village and center for activities on the water located on Kaageiland (Kaag Island) is a good base for walks through the village or across the fields to a traditional windmill.

The Kaagerplassen surrounds Kaageiland on east, south and west sides, an area of lakes, islands and channels used by watersports enthusiasts of all types. There are many secluded coves for a private anchorage; several channels at the northern end of the Kagerplassen connect to the Ringvaart. From the south it is just 3km from Leiden to the first of the Kaag lakes. The lakes are big enough to get a little choppy; for an overnight mooring there is a protected spot inside an island on the Balgerij, a narrow cut at the north end of the lake with access to the Ringvaart.

Jachthaven Kaagdorp	jachthavenkaagdorp.nl	0612 202 881
Jachthaven 't Fissertje	sloepenopdekaag.nl	0252 545 107
Kon.WV De Kaag	www.kwvdekaag.nl	071 30 10 035
Jachthaven De Horizon		0715 018 503

The Ringvaart is crossed by relatively few highway or railway bridges; some of the bridges are high enough to allow mastless boats to pass under. They do open when necessary, check the schedule. The bridge at Cruquius (above), 16km north from Kaag, is the landmark to turn north onto the river Spaarne; the junction is a few hundred meters east of the bridge. Below is the Leimuiderbrug, at the western tip of the Westeinder Plassen; it marks the border between Noord Holland and Zuid Holland.

Haarlem

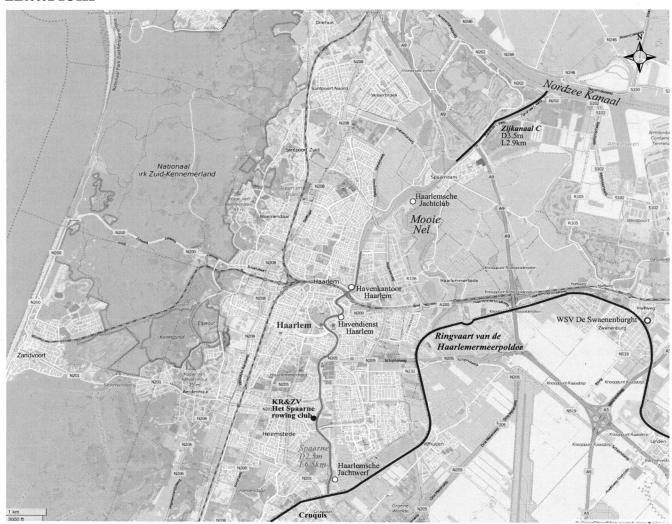

The city of Haarlem is an easy excursion from the Ringvaart, via the Spaarne river. It flows freely into the center of Haarlem as a true river. Current is not significant but the twisting path and natural, irregular shoreline make the sightseeing very pleasant. For the first kilometer above the Ringvaart green fields come right to the water on the west side. The east side is a continuous line of moored boats and houseboats. The city begins as you pass under a bridge and perhaps encounter rowing shells from the dock of the KRZV Het Spaarne, the local "royal rowing & sailing club".

Boats often gather to wait at these two drawbridges on busy streets leading into the city center. The river makes S-turns as it cuts through the city. There are two more drawbridges, then the footbridge Gravestenenbrug, followed by five more BB drawbridges. The river Spaarne then widens into lakes before connecting through a lock into Zijkanaal C at Spaarndam, leading to the Nordzee Kanaal with access to the North Sea, Amsterdam or Nord Holland canals.

Haarlem

The Gravestenenbrug mooring quay (above, beyond the bridge) is at a central location; the nearby footbridge gives good access to the heart of the city, on the west side. The market square, church and many restaurants and shops are only two blocks away. The former bridgekeeper's quarters are in the small brick building (at the western end of the bridge, labeled Douche Gravestenenbrug) that is now the base for a large sculpture of the winged foot of Mercury; showers for boaters are inside.

The Grote Kerk van St. Bavo dominates the market square; inside is one of the most stunning church organs in Holland, a Muller that was constructed in 1738. It's over 90 ft. high and has more than 5000 pipes. Both Handel and Mozart played it, the latter when he was only 10.

This is generally a city to live in, not a tourist destination. It is the capital of Noord Holland province (rather than Amsterdam, as one might think.) The city is only a few kilometers behind the sand dunes of the North Sea at Zandvoort, one of the most popular beaches in Holland.

A fee is due for the use of the waterway and for overnight mooring. At the northern edge of the city is the Havenkantoor, the office of the Havendienst (port authority) responsible for city moorings. It is just over one km north of Gravestenenbrug, a long blue box building set on pilings on the west bank.

Westeinderplassen

This lake, with its many jachthavens, is accessible only along its west shore, which is formed by the Ringvaart van de Haarlemmeerpolder. Access channels are via Wijde Gat or Vaarsloot. There are about sixty marinas, boat clubs, boat yards and other marine services on the Westeinderplassen, most of them in the northwestern corner along scores of small canals with access to the lake or Ringvaart.

For the full list of places and descriptions go to:
www.aalsmeerwesteinder.nl

Ringvaart near Vaarsloot

Braassemermeer/ Woubrugge

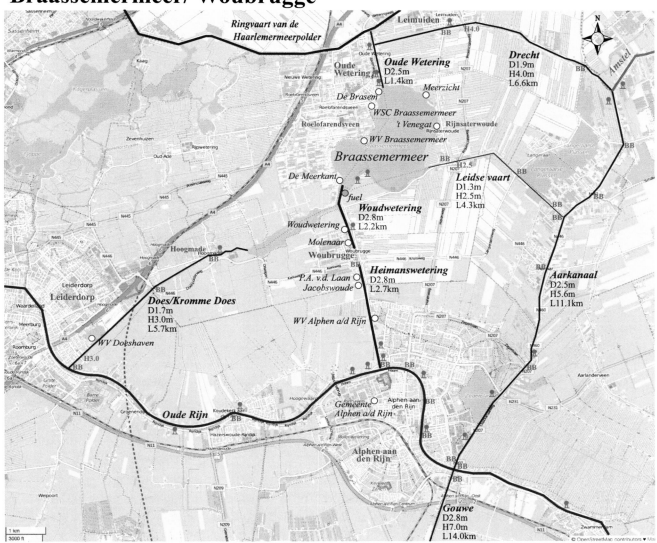

Visiting boaters are welcome at WV Braassemermeer:
Passersby are welcome! Do you want to meet for a coffee, meet for lunch or a drink on the boardwalk, put into the outer jetty. That's so easy, safe and you have a good view of your vessel. Do you want to stay longer or overnight for example, then sail into the harbor. You can moor at the passers dock you see immediately to port.

WV Braassemermeer	braassemermeer.nl	0713 312 326
WSC Braassemermeer	jachthaven-wb.nl	0713 314 002
Jachthaven De Brasem	www.jachthavendebrasem.nl	0713 312 664
Jachthaven Meerzicht	gebrweinholt.nl	0172 508 204

Jachthaven Woudwetering www.jachthavenwoudwetering.nl 06 43 67 24 50
Jachthaven De Meerkant   0171 3314 676
Yacht charter base/jachthaven/service P.A.Van der Laan www.laanyacht.nl   0172 518 113

Heart of Holland - Purple Tour

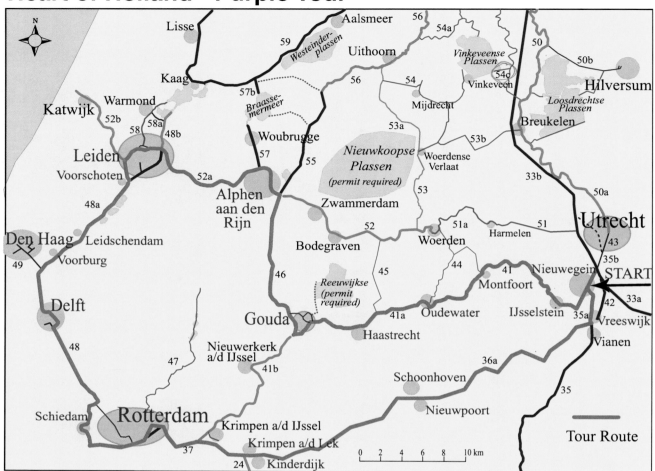

This loop around the southern side of the Heart of Holland includes the Lek and Nieuwe Maas rivers, one of the major branches of the Rhine. However, these rivers are very busy with barge traffic and can have strong current; recommended only for experienced skippers. The route offers a vist to the large city of Rotterdam and an excursion for a day at the beach, if you wish.

Day 1 - The tour route starts at Nieuwegein, a suburb of Utrecht, on the Merwede Kanaal. Travel south from there to the Lek; stop for a tour of the old canal in Vreeswijk, then on to Schoonhoven for lunch and sightseeing. Overnight at Rotterdam.

Day 2 - Visit Rotterdam, then on to Delft in the afternoon. Stop overnight on the south of Delft.

Day 3 - Visit Den Haag if desired, then overnight at Leiden passantenhaven.

Day 4 - Spend the day touring Leiden or at the beach of Katwijk.

Day 5 - Travel east to Gouda for an afternoon and overnight visit.

Day 6 - Return on the Hollandse IJsel river, with stops at Oudewater and Montfoort.

Purple Tour: Nieuwegein - Schoonhoven - Rotterdam - Delft - Leiden - Gouda

WATERWAY Names are as shown on ANWB charts	FROM	TO	KM	LOCKS	BRIDGES to open	DEPTH minimum	WIDTH locks/ bridges	HEIGHT fixed bridges	TRAVEL TIME hours
Merwedekanaal	Nieuwegein	Vreeswijk	3.0	1	3	3.1	9.0	none	
Lek river	Vreeswijk	Schoonhoven	22.6	0	0	varies	open	13.5	
Lek river	Schoonhoven	Krimpen a/d Lek	17.5	0	0	varies	open	none	
Nieuwe Maas river	Krimpen a/d Lek	Rotterdam	12.0	0	0	6.0	50.0	3.7	
Day 1		**Rotterdam**	55.1	1	3	3.1	9.0	3.7	6.0
Deltse Schiekanaal	Rotterdam	Delft	9.0	1	11	2.3	7.8	none	
Day 2		**Delft**	9.0	1	11	2.3	7.8	none	2.0
Rijn Schiekanaal	Delft	Den Haag	12.2	2	5	1.9	6.0	none	
Rijn Schiekanaal	Den Haag	Leiden	17.8	1	11	2.8	6.3	5.6	
Day 3		**Leiden**	30.0	3	16	1.9	6.0	5.6	6.0
Nieuwe Vaart	Leiden	Korte Vlietkanaal	5.5	0	6	2.8	8.0	none	
Korte Vlietkanaal	Rijn Schiekanaal	Oude Rijn	2.0	0	3	3.3	10.5	none	
Oude Rijn	Korte Vlietkanaal	Katwijk	8.5	0	7	2.9	8.4	none	
Day 4		**Katwijk -return Leiden**	32.0	0	16	2.8	8.0	none	3.5
Oude Rijn	Leiden	Alphen aan den Rijn	16.5	0	9	2.5	10.0	none	
Gouwe	Alphen aan den Rijn	Nieuwe Gouwe	14.7	0	6	2.8	14.0	none	
Nieuwe Gouwe	Gouwe	Gouda	1.5	1	2	2.4	9.0	none	
Day 5		**Gouda**	32.7	1	17	2.4	9.0	none	5.0
Hollandse IJssel river	Gouda	IJsselstein	32.0	2	10	1.7	6.0	4.7	
Doorslag	IJsselstein	Nieuwegein	2.2	1	2	1.7	5.8	4.4	
Day 6		**Nieuwegein**	34.2	3	12	1.7	5.8	4.4	8.0
TOTAL			193.0	9	75	1.7	5.8	3.7	30.5

Lek River

As the Nieuwe Maas river becomes the Lek and the Hollandse IJssel river branches northeastward, Kinderdijk is the first landmark on right-side bank. It is the largest group of old windmills in NL. The 19 molens were built around 1740 to drain the polder. There is no mooring on the south bank near the site but there are two marinas on the north bank and a ferry for access.

Nieuwpoort: A well-preserved star fort town directly on the south bank of the Lek, this can be an interesting short stop for a return to the 17th century. The canal is no longer in use but it provides a walkway through the center of town and a return via the dikes of the star-shaped walls along the singel.

> WSV Nova Portus   0619 716 596

Schoonhoven: Just across the river on the north bank, this is the historic "Silver Town" of Holland. Shops and craftsmen are located throughout the old district, especially in the Watertower, an often-photographed building.

> Gemente Schoonhoven www.krimpenerwaard.nl   0648 131 833
> WV De Zilverloot   www.wsvdezilvervloot.nl   06 23 91 51 94

Vreeswijk: A short (20km) section of the Lek leads from Nieuwpoort/Schoonhoven to Vreeswijk and a turn north onto Merwede Kanaal. Vreeswijk is an historic barging center because of its central location. A section of the old river branch Vaartse Rijn, now with boat access from the river blocked by a flood gate and fixed bridge, passes through the center of town. Water traffic uses Merwedekanaal on the west side or the Lekkanaal on the east, which is the wider, straighter canal used by barges. Visit the historic barge shipyard museum. www.museumwerf.nl

> Vianen: WSV De Peiler www.depeiler.nl   0622 850 854

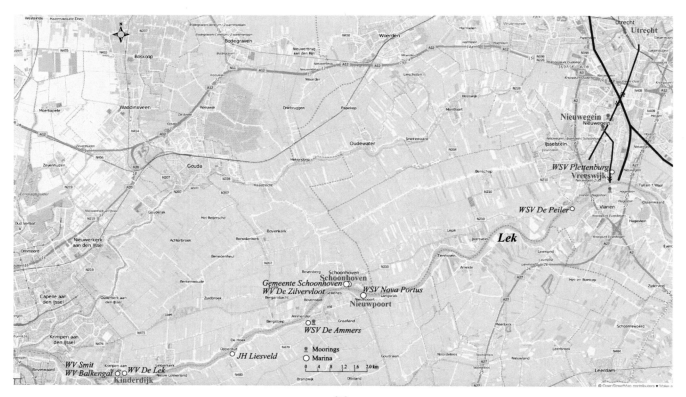

Rotterdam and Schiedam

Rotterdam: This modern and architecturally innovative city has risen from almost total destruction from the bombings of 1940. Spread along both sides of the Nieuwe Maas are the docks and industrial haven of the largest port in Europe. Despite the busy waterways, leisure boats can easily avoid the commercial traffic and find a comfortable mooring to visit the city. The Veerhaven, just west of the Erasmus bridge, is convenient to the center of the city, Museum Park and the Euromast with its top-rated restaurant and views across the city. Delfshaven, two kilometers further west, was built in the 14th century to give the city of Delft canal access to the river Maas. It is a quiet, cosy and offers several waterfront cafes. City Marina, on the south side of the river near the Willemsbrug, is the largest and has the most services.

Veerhaven Rotterdam www.veerhavenrotterdam.nl   06 24 35 19 27

City Marina Rotterdam www.rotterdammarina.nl   0104 85 40 96

Schiedam: Although it is adjacent to Rotterdam, this small city was not destroyed by the bombing of WWII. The old city center is ringed by canals; five working grain mills supply the remaining jenever (gin) distilleries, of the hundreds which once were the main business of Schiedam. Moorings can be found at several places along the canals or in marinas off the river or near the city center. www.schiedam.nl

Jachtclub Schiedam (Spuihaven) www.jachtclubschiedam.nl   06 44 32 67 22

WV De Nieuwe Haven www.wsvdenieuwehaven.nl 06 57 46 20 92

Yacht Broker: Doeve Brokers www.doevemakelaar.nl 0102 48 98 30

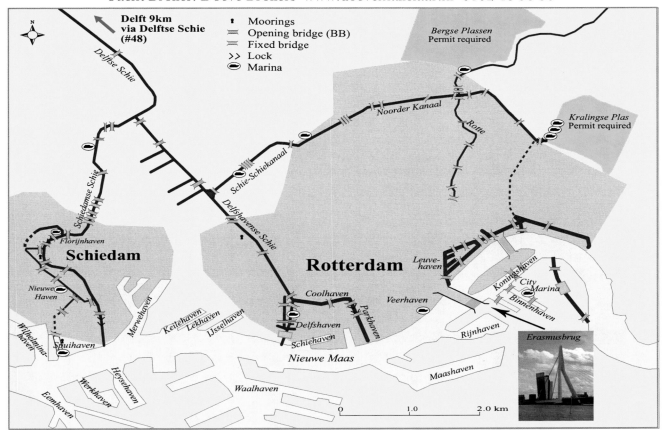

Rotterdam/Schiedam
To Delft/Den Haag

The map at right shows the connections to Delft from the Nieuwe Maas river, through Schiedam or Rotterdam, and then north to Den Haag or on to Leiden on the Rijn-Schiekanaal.

Alternately, the route could return east to the Heart of Holland waterways at Gouda via the Nieuwe Maas & Hollandse IJssel river.

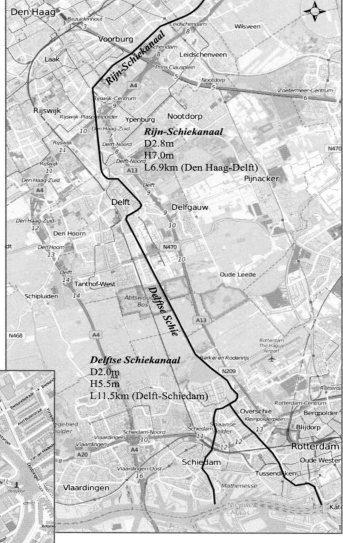

Rijn-Schiekanaal
D2.8m
H7.0m
L6.9km (Den Haag-Delft)

Delftse Schiekanaal
D2.0m
H5.5m
L11.5km (Delft-Schiedam)

For more information on visiting Delft go to:
www.delft.nl/delften/Tourists

Delft

The tourist office states "Delft is a town abounding in water." It's true, there are canals throughout the city, one of them used only by permanent houseboats. But when you arrive in Delft on your own boat you cannot use these canals. You must bypass the old town center along its eastern side on the Rijn-Schiekanaal and stay at the only mooring place, Zuid Kolk, for 24 hours or less. The Zuid Kolk haven is at the southern end of the town, a triangular enlargement of the canal intersection, part of the original singel surrounding the town. The singel on the west side has been replaced by a street and rail lines. Local small boats are moored along the Buitenwatersloot, a very pretty canal to walk or visit by dinghy from the Zuid Kolk. It is lined by trees, shrubs and on both sides; waterlilies grow between the boats. Many of the boats and the houses are charming

From the south, the Delftse Schie is a straight-line approach from Rotterdam. At the Zuid Kolk the through route makes a 90-degree turn to the east, becoming the Delftse Vliet of Rijn-Schiekanaal, then two more turns bring it back onto the original path at the north end of town. The canals within the historical town centre are of course a good way to walk and see the sights, or you can go on a canal tourboat or step into the Canalhopper (water taxi).

The Oostpoort (East Gate, in photo), built around 1400, is a picturesque sight. From the Zuid Kolk mooring walk south one block on the Hooikade quay, then across a bridge over the Delftse Schie to the Royal Delft porcelain factory on Rotterdamsweg for demonstrations and a factory shop. www.royaldelft.com

Continue along the canal east bank to the Oostpoort, then cross back to the Oosteinde canal quay, which leads right to the heart of the old city. This canal has lots of water lilies, it is a pleasant walking route. White-railing footbridges cross the canal at frequent intervals.

The slender tower of the Nieuwe Kerk (New Church, 1381) shoots up almost 109 metres from its location on the Markt, opposite the town hall. The royal tomb in the church has long been the last resting place for the members of the Royal House. There are views to Den Haag and Rotterdam from the tower.

There are many outdoor cafes on the Markt, the largest market square in the Netherlands, between the town hall and the Nieuwe Kerk. Also visit those on the lively Beestenmarkt square, two blocks to the south. This perfectly-square block is notable for its complete coverage by leafy trees and the many indoor and outdoor cafes which line all four sides.

Den Haag

The Rijn-Schiekanaal leads south from Leiden to Leidschendam, a suburb of Den Haag (The Hague.) This is a good place to stop overnight; a bus route leads into Den Haag, for a visit to the museums, shops and restaurants. Or sail right into the center of the city and moor on the Bierkade at the docks of De Ooievaart (shown below), subject to limits of 2.9m height and 1.7m depth in the canals. Moorings along the Laakhaven are just a few blocks further away from the center.

Holland's most famous seaside resort, Scheveningen, is just at the west of Den Haag. Canals reach to the beach harbor but through-passage is closed for boats on the inland waterways.
The royal painting collection, at the Mauritshuis, is one of the best in the world; it includes works by Rembrandt and Vermeer.

Museums in Den Haag include:

Gemeente Museum
www.gemeentemuseum.nl/

Mauritshuis museum
www.mauritshuis.nl/en/

Leiden

The approximately 6.5km-long outer singel ring of Leiden is still intact, although the old walls and bastions are now mainly greenery. There are parks and an old cemetery in the star points. A special walk is the Witte Singel pathway around the botanical gardens and the Observatory, at the south-western-most corner of the singel. (see Leiden city map on page 69)

The island between the Oude Rijn and Nieuwe Rijn, bounded on the east by Zijlsingel, is one of the most undisturbed bits of Leiden. The canals are narrow, the trees and flowers are plentiful and the houses are charming.This is a place to stroll around, just enjoying the Dutch way of life.

Walk along the curve of the Nieuwe Rijn almost to the point where it meets the Oude Rijn, watching for a narrow alley named Burgsteeg; this leads to the walls of De Burcht, a circular fortress atop an earthen mound, centrally located in the city. Walk around its ramparts to gain a full view of the city.

If you are in Holland without a boat, or want a smaller boat for a day cruise, the Leiden canals or lakes of Kaagerplassen are perfect for a day trip; rent an open sloep from Olympia: www.olympia-charters.nl/en/daycruiser-charter/boat-rental-kaag/

Gouda

Vessels arriving from the north on the Gouwekanaal can enter Gouda on the Nieuwe Gouwe to the boat club WV Gouda (left) or continue on for moorings along the canals.

WV Gouda   0614 884 345
www.watersportvereniging-gouda.nl

To bypass Gouda and join the Hollandse IJssel river use one of the side-by-side chambers of the Julianasluis (below.)

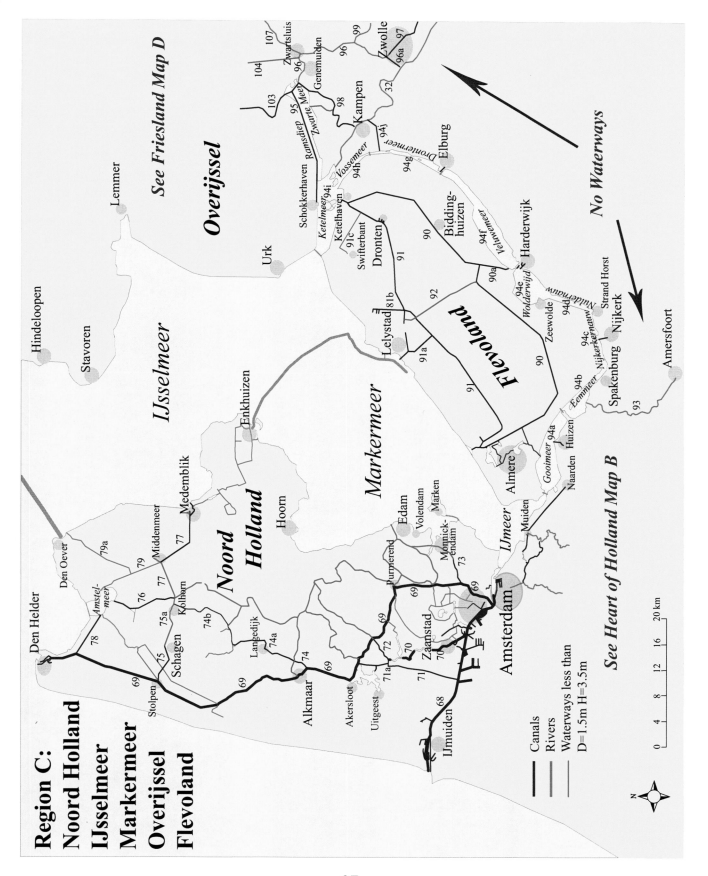

Region C:
Noord Holland
IJsselmeer
Markermeer
Overijssel
Flevoland

Den Helder

Den Oever

Lemmer

Hindeloopen

Stavoren

See Friesland Map D

Overijssel

IJsselmeer

Zwartsluis
Zwolle
Zwartsluis
96
Genemuiden
107
104
103
95
Ramsdiep
Zwarte Meer
98
Kampen
32
99
96
97
96a
94j

Urk

Schokkerhaven
Ketelmeer 94i
Ketelhaven
Vossemeer
94h
Dronten
91c
Swifterbant
91
90
Elburg
94g
Biddinghuizen
94f
Veluwemeer
Harderwijk
Dronter meer

Noord
Holland

Medemblik
Middenmeer
79a
79
77
77
76
75a
Kollhorn
78
Amstel-meer
Stolpen
75
Schagen
74b
Langedijk
74a
69
74
Alkmaar
Akersloot
Uitgeest
71a
Enkhuizen

Hoorn

Markermeer

Lelystad
81b
92
91
90a
90
91
91
91a
Zeewolde
94e
Wolderwijd
Nuldernauw
94d
Strand Horst
94c
Nijkernauw
Nijkerk
Spakenburg
93
Amersfoort

Flevoland

No Waterways

Purmerend
Edam
Volendam
Marken
Monnick-endam
73
72
71
70
70a
70
Zaanstad
69
69
69
69
68
IJmuiden
Amsterdam
IJmeer
Muiden
Almere
Naarden
Huizen
94a
Gooimeer
94b
Eemmeer

See Heart of Holland Map B

Canals
Rivers
Waterways less than
D=1.5m H=3.5m

N

0   4   8   12   16   20 km

WATERWAY	MAP	FROM	TO	KM LONG	No. of LOCKS	LOCK SIZE	DRAFT meters	HEIGHT meters
Noordhollandschkanaal	69	Noordzeekanaal	Den Helder	79.0	3	5.3X49.0	2.80	6.80
Zaan (river) & Zijkanaal G	70	Noordzeekanaal	Knollendammer Vaart	13.0	1	11.5X120	3.0 m	BB
Nauernaschevaart & Zijkanaal D	71	Noordzeekanaal	Tapsloot	9.0	1	5.6X27.0	2.00	BB
Tapsloot	71a	Nauernaschevaart	Zaan	1.0	0		3.00	BB
Knollendammer Vaart	72	Zaan	Noordzeekanaal	4.0	0		2.00	BB
Trekvaart Het Schouw	73	Noordhollanschkanaal	Monnickendam	8.0	2	6.0X43.7	1.30	3.90
Knl. Omval-Kolhorn/Kraspolder Knl.	74	Alkmaar	Huigen Vaart	2.0	0		2.50	4.80
Knl. Omval-Kolhorn/Langedijker Vaart	74a	Huigen Vaart	Het Waartje	12.0	1	6.6X50.0	2.50	3.50
Knl. Omval-Kolhorn/Niedorper Knl.	74b	Het Waartje	Kolhorn	16.0	1	6.6X50.0	2.60	3.60
Knl. Stolpen-Schagen	75	Stolpen	Schagen	4.0	0		2.50	BB
Knl. Schagen-Kolhorn	75a	Schagen	Kolhorn	8.0	1	6.9X40.0	2.60	2.90
Waardkanaal	76	Kolhorn	Amstelmeer	9.0	0		3.60	BB
Westfriesevaart	77	Kolhorn	Middenmeer	18.0	3	7.0X39.0	3.00	7.20
Balgzandkanaal	78	Noordhollanschkanaal	Amstelmeer	6.0	1	10.0X70.0	3.40	BB
Slootvaart	79	Middenmeer	Amstelmeer	9.0	1	7.0X33.2	1.50	5.60
Den Oeversevaart	79a	Slootvaart	Den Oever	14.0	1	5.6X31.2	1.50	3.80
Hoge Vaart	90	Almere	Ketelhaven	62.0	2	6.6X43.0	2.40	5.40
Hoge Dwarsvaart	90a	Hoge Vaart	Harderwijk	4.0	1	5.0X20.0	2.10	3.90
Lage Vaart	91	Almere	Ketelhaven	48.0	2	7.4X62.0	2.40	6.50
Lage Dwarsvaart	91a	Markermeer	Lage Vaart	6.0	1	8.2X63.0	2.40	6.50
Oostervaart	91b	Lage Vaart	Oostervaart	4.0	0		2.30	open
Swiftervaart	91c	Lage Vaart	Swifterbant	7.0	0		1.10	4.30
Larservaart	92	Lage Vaart	Hoge Vaart	12.0	1	5.0X22.0	1.70	3.00
Eem river	93	Eemmeer	Amersfoort	18.0	0		3.00	7.20

WATERWAY	MAP	FROM	TO	KM LONG	No. of LOCKS	LOCK SIZE	DRAFT	HEIGHT
Randmeren: Gooimeer	94a	Hollandsebrug	Stichtsebrug	14.0	0		2.80	12.90
Randmeren: Eemmeer	94b	Stichtsebrug	Spakenburg	9.0	0		2.80	12.90
Randmeren: Nijkerkernauw	94c	Spakenburg	Nulde	9.0	1	10.0X90.0	2.80	BB
Randmeren: Nuldernauw	94d	Nulde	Strand Horst	11.0	0		2.80	open
Randmeren: Wolderwijd	94e	Strand Horst	Harderwijk	15.0	0		2.80	open
Randmeren: Veluwemeer	94f	Harderwijk	Elburg	19.0	0		2.80	BB
Randmeren: Drontermeer	94g	Elburg	Roggebotsluis	11.0	1	10.0X90.0	3.20	open
Randmeren: Vossemeer	94h	Roggebotsluis	Ketelhaven	8.0	0		2.80	5.60
Randmeren: Ketelmeer	94i	Ketelhaven	Ketelbrug	9.0	0		2.90	open
Randmeren: Reevediep	94j	Randmeren	IJssel river	8.0	1	10.0X70.0	n/a	n/a
Ramsdiep/Zwarte Meer	95	Schokkerstrand	Zwarte Water	17.0	0		3.10	open
Zwarte Water	96	Vollenhoverkanaal/	Z Zwolle	22.0	0		3.30	5.50
Zwolle-IJsselkanaal	96a	Zwolle	IJssel river	3.0	1	14.0X142	4.75	BB
Nieuwe Wetering	97	Zwarte Water	Zwolle	2.0	0		3.00	BB
Ganzendiep	98	Kampen	Geenemuiden	12.0	1	5.8X32.0	1.80	5.00
Overijsselse Vecht	99	Zwarte Water	Junne near Ommen	33.0	2	6.0X36.0	1.70	3.30
Kadoeler Meer/Zwanendiep	103	Zwarte Meer	Vollenhove	7.0	0		2.80	BB2.6
Arembergergracht	104	Zwartsluis	Beulaker Wijde	8.0	1	4.45X27.8	1.40	BB3.5
Meppelerdiep	107	Zwartsluis	Meppel	10.0	0		3.50	open

Noord Holland - Tan Tour

This is a short tour of the southern part of Noord Holland province. Along with a visit to the charming town of Alkmaar it includes the seaport towns of Edam, Volendam and Monnickendam, without the need to enter the busy and sometimes choppy waters of the Markermeer. Or those towns can be bypassed via the Noordhollandschkanaal at Purmerend.

The tour can begin from Amsterdam or from Haarlem via the Sparne river, Zijkanaal C and the Nordzeekanaal.

Tan tour: Amsterdam - Alkmaar - Purmerend - Edam - Monnickendam - Marken

WATERWAY Names as shown on ANWB charts	FROM	TO	KM	LOCKS	BRIDGES to open	DEPTH minimum	WIDTH locks/ bridges	HEIGHT fixed bridges	TRAVEL TIME hours
Noordzeekanaal	Amsterdam	Zaandam	6.6	0	0	11.0	open	none	
Zijkanaal G	Noordzeekanaal	Zaanseschans	7.0	1	6	3.0	11.5	6.5	
Zaan river	Zaanseschans	West-Knollendam	6.4	0	3	3.0	12.0	none	
Markervaart	West-Knollendam	De Woude	4.6	0	1	2.1	14.0	none	
Kogerpolderkanaal	De Woude	Gat op de Meer	2.7	0	0	3.0	open	none	
Noordhollandschkanaal	Gat op de Meer	Alkmaar	7.5	0	0	3.5	open	none	
Day 1		Alkmaar	34.8		10	2.1	11.5	none	5.0
Noordhollandschkanaal	Alkmaar	Gat op de Meer	7.5	0	0	3.5	open	none	
Kogerpolderkanaal	Gat op de Meer	De Woude	2.7	0	0	3.0	open	none	
Vinkenhop	De Woude	Spijkerboor	4.5	0	0	3.0	15.5	4.5	
Noordhollandschkanaal	Spijkerboor	Purmerend	8.8	0	0	3.0	27.0	6.9	
Day 2		Purmerend	23.5		0	3.0	15.5	5.3	4.0
Where	Noordhollandschkanaal	Purmer ringvaart	2.2	0	5	1.5	6.3	none	
Where	Purmer ringvaart	Edam	6.8	0	2	1.6	5.6	2.9	
Day 3		Edam	9.0		7	1.5	5.6	none	1.5
Monnickendam-Edam	Edam	Stinkevuil of Purmer Ee	4.8	0	0	1.0	24.0	3.2	
Stinkevuil of Purmer Ee	Monnickendam-Edam	Monnickendam	2.0	1	5	2.5	6.6	3.7	
Gouwzee	Monnickendam	Marken island	4.5	0	0	2.0	open	none	
Gouwzee	Marken island	Monnickendam	4.5	0	0	2.0	open	none	
Day 4		Monnickendam	15.8		5	1.0	6.6	3.2	3.0
Monnickendam-Edam	Monnickendam	Broek in Waterland	4.8	2	2	1.1	6.4	none	
Trekvaart Het Schouw	Broek in Waterland	Noordhollandschkanaal	3.4	0	1	1.8	7.9	3.9	
Noordhollandschkanaal	Het Schouw	Amsterdam	6.3	1	4	3.0	15.0	7.0	
Day 5		Amsterdam	14.5	0	7	1.1	6.4	3.9	2.5
TOTAL			97.6	0	29	1.0	6.4	3.2	16.0

Noord Holland - Tan Tour

The tour begins in the major metropolitan area of Amsterdam/Zaanstad but soon the surroundings open into the wide spaces of the Noord Holland peninsula. The Noordhollandskanaal continues on to the tip of the peninsula at Den Helder, where there is access to the North Sea or the Waddenzee; the latter offers a crossing to Friesland at Harlingen. But many consider the trip north to be boring and stop at Alkmaar before returning to Amsterdam.

Zaandam, Koog a/d Zaan and Zaandijk are all part of the municipality of Zaanstad, a mostly-residential extension of Amsterdam spread along the Zaan river. The area is a combination of the new and the old, with few points of interest but good shopping from free moorings.

Zaanse Schans, on the east bank of the river just at the northern end of the metropolitan area, is an openair museum of traditional buildings and working windmills. Moorings are available but are often crowded.

De Woude offers plentiful free moorings along the canal banks. There are no services except the restaurant 't Kombof on the west side. This is a good base for a bicycle excursion (10km round-trip) to De Rijp, a classic Dutch village with a highly-rated restaurant, Het Wapen van Munster.

Alkmaar is the destination of this tour, a medieval town offering a famous cheese market on Fridays in the summer. The narrow lanes are ideal for walking or cycling tours, or the small canals can be traveled by dinghy or tourist boats. *Bierkade* is the long quay on the west bank of the canal, marked by the beautiful *Accijnstoren* tower at its southern end; check in here for a berth assignment.

Gemeente Alkmaar www.havensinalkmaar.nl   0725 20 00 14
Jachtwerf Nicolaas Witsen (boatyard) www.nicolaaswitsen.nl   0725 11 22 97
Service: Allard Benjamins info@abys.nl   06 51 21 12 33

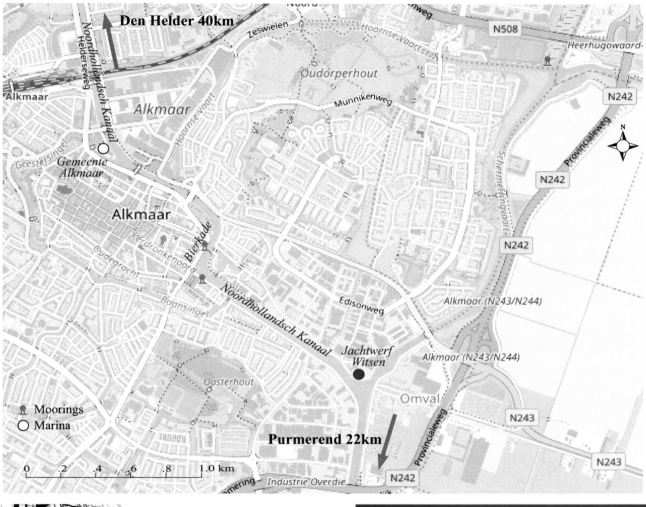

Purmerend is the main trading town of Waterland, the low area with hundreds of drainage canals begun 500 years ago. These flatlands cover Noord Holland north from Amsterdam and west from the IJsselmeer to beyond the Zaan river. The streets of the old town center of Purmerend include a wide range of shops; moorings are located nearby, on the Noordhollandschkanaal.

Gemeente Purmerend www.purmerend.nl 06 10 15 08 57

WSV Purmerend 06 10 15 08 57

Edam means cheese to most of the world; multilingual commentary for tourists accompanies the recreated bartering between farmers and merchants in the town square every Wednesday in July and August.

Boaters arriving on this tour will pass by classic lifting bridges and the perfectly-kept, charming residences and shops of this famous town. Moorings along a grassy park are available at the Nieuwe Haven. Travel by bicycle or bus to the even more tourist-visited port of Volendam, a recreated fishing village with dockside restaurants and shops.

Volendam (Nieuwe Haven)

0299 37 14 77 or 06 22 51 52 10

Monnickendam is a major recreational harbor on the west coast of the IJsselmeer; the marinas and the waterfront are oriented to the inland sea rather than the canals. This port offers access from Amsterdam to the IJsselmeer while bypassing the huge and busy commercial Oranjesluizen locks. It is a short protected run across the Gouwzee to Marken island, another old fishing port and a good place for hiking to view the old cottages along the seashore.

Gemeente Waterland www.waterland.nl 0299 65 55 67

WSV Marken 0299 60 13 82

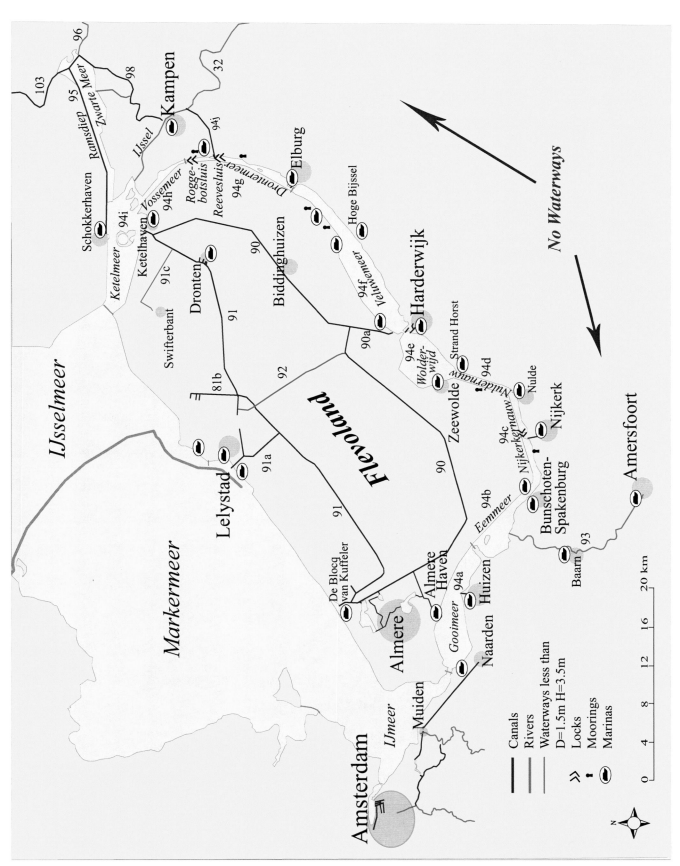

Amsterdam

IJmeer

Muiden

Markermeer

IJsselmeer

Lelystad

Swifterbant

Schokkerhaven

Ketelmeer

94i

Ketelhaven

Vossemeer

94h

Rogge-botsluis

Reevesluis

94j

Kampen

95 *Ramsdiep*

Zwarte Meer

98

IJssel

96

103

32

91c

Dronten

90

Biddinghuizen

94g

Dronтермeer

Elburg

Hoge Bijssel

94f

Veluwemeer

Harderwijk

90a

94e

Wolder-wijd

Strand Horst

Nuldernauw

94d

Nulde

Zeewolde

90

94c

Nijkerk

Nijkerkernauw

Bunschoten-Spakenburg

94b

Eemmeer

Baarn

93

Amersfoort

91

92

81b

91a

De Blocq van Kuffeler

Almere Haven

94a

Gooimeer

Almere

Naarden Huizen

Flevoland

No Waterways

Canals

Rivers

Waterways less than D=1.5m H=3.5m

Locks

Moorings

Marinas

N

0   4   8   12   16   20 km

Randmeren van Flevoland

The internal canals of Flevoland, Lage Vaart and Hoge Vaart, provide a protected route along the southeastern shore of the Markermeer, peaceful waterways that are often lined with forests. However the passage through the lakes that line the south and east of the polder is a more popular route between central Holland and Friesland, with many mooring choices and several interesting towns to visit.

Naarden A large marina on the Gooimeer is just over 2km from the old city, the most spectacular of the "Star Fort" towns of the Netherlands. The 12-point dual moat fortifications are still intact and can be seen via classic tour boats or from the St Vituskerk tower. The well-preserved town is now a center for upscale shopping. There are plans to link the Naardertrekvaart to the Gooimeer in the future but at present there is no waterway connection.

Jachthaven Naarden www.jachthavennaarden.nl 0356 95 60 50

Shipshape Jachtservice Gooimeer 0359 94 78 59

Almere Haven is the waterfront section of the reidential southwestern tip of the Flevoland polder. The area has become populated only since the late 1950s and thus is far different than the classic Dutch towns. Theme restaurants line the harbor quay, with modern shopping just behind. Boats requiring less than 2.5 meters bridge clearance can enter the canal system of the polder from this harbor.

WSV Almere Haven www.wsvalmerehaven.nl 0365 31 75 17

Gemeentehaven Almere www.almere.nl 0365 47 18 22

Huizen is old fishing port that has become highly industrialized. There are marinas and municipal moorings but the town offers little of interest, especially as compared to the other towns described on this page.

Jachthaven Huizen www.jachthavenhuizen.nl   0355 25 86 22

Gemeentehaven Huizen www.huizenhavenvantgooi.nl   0355 28 12 22

Huizer Marina www.huizermarina.nl   0355 25 11 59

Miechiel Zwiebel Totaal Jachtservice   0355 25 44 98

Amersfoort (via river Eem) lies 18 kilometers south of the Gooimeer along a winding river through quiet rural countryside. Amersfoort is a town with an amazing juxtaposition of the new and the old. A new municipal dock with all the necessities (electricity, water, showers and welcoming personnel) opened in 2007, a short walk upriver from the town gate (shown below).

Gemeente Amersfoort www.eemhavenamersfoort.nl   033 46 95 070

Jachthaven De Stuw www.jachthavendestuw.nl   0334 72 10 06

WV De Eemkruisers www.eemkruisers.nl   06 54 11 17 68

Jachtwerf De Eem Elzenaars 0334 80 36 91

Bunschoten-Spakenburg: When the Dutch closed off the Zuider Zee with dikes, they essentially put small fishing villages out of business. It was either find something else to do or die. Small villages like Spakenburg found salvation in tourism. On view are the typical fishing boats of the area, called "botters", lying in the harbor or on the slipways in a museumboatyard. Local culture and history is celebrated in events throughout the summer, when women wear traditional clothes.

      Gemeente Bunschoten www.bunschoten.nl   06 30 29 19 75

      WSV De Eendracht www.wsvdeeendracht.nl   06 53 12 66 33

Nijkerk (4 km via Arkervaart) is an ordinary town, which has been modernized and industrialized throughout.   Gemeente Nijkerk www.nijkerk.org 0332 45 12 07

Nulde and **Strand Horst** are large modern marinas in a natural setting, no town nearby but with access to sandy beaches.

      Jachthaven Nulde www.wsvnulde.nl   06 13 29 42 10

      Jachthaven Strand Horst www.strandhorst.com   0341 56 13 33

Harderwijk: In the 13th century this town was an important trading port on the Zuider Zee, but silting and the eventual making of the Flevoland polder has turned it into a popular stop on the inland Randmeren route. It is a beautifully preserved town, blending the old and new in a pleasant manner. The rail station offers frequent service either north or southbound. The major tourist attraction is the Dophinarium, the largest sea-zoo in Europe. There are plentiful moorings in the centrally-located municipal Visserhaven or marinas.

      Gemeente Harderwijk www.harderwijk.nl   0341 41 13 39

      Jachthaven De Knar www.wvflevo.nl 0341 42 32 71

      Service: Eerland Scheepstechniek 0341 41 53 73

      Service: Holland Marine Service www.hmsboten.nl 0320 28 81 99

Elburg is another fortress town, this one with rectangular fortifications and moat. The original town is well preserved and offers a weekly street market, several nice restaurants and a full range of shopping. The extensive boating service community is focused on leisure vessels.

      Gemeente Elburg www.elburg.nl 0525 688 688

      Jachtcenter Elburg www.jachtcenter.nl 0525 68 28 00

Reevediep: As of October 2019, Roggebotsluis is no longer in service, replaced by Reevesluis, an entirely new lock located 2.8km south. A new channel, Reevediep (#94j), has been created north of the lock to connect from the Drontemeer east to the river IJssel south of Kampen. The primary purpose of the new channel is to manage water flow from the IJssel river to the IJsselmeer, but it can also be a useful connection for boaters.

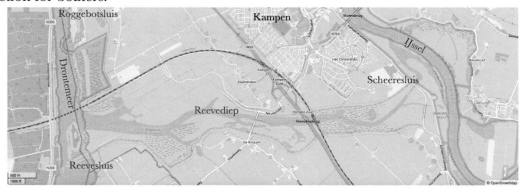

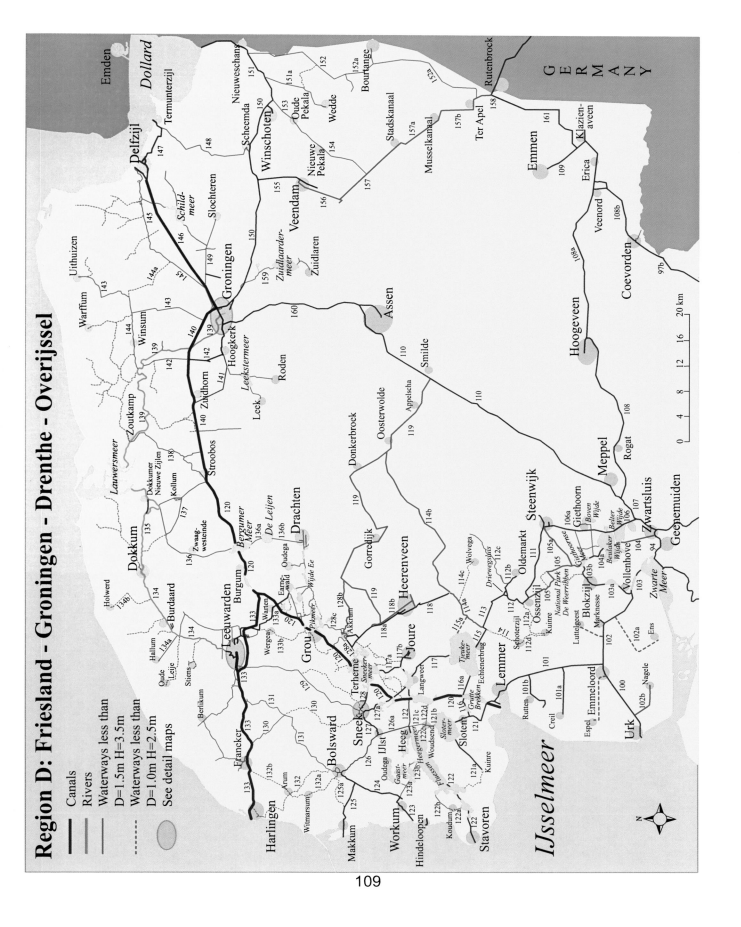

Region D: Friesland - Groningen - Drenthe - Overijssel

Canals
Rivers
Waterways less than
D=1.5m H=3.5m
Waterways less than
D=1.0m H=2.5m
See detail maps

Dollard

Emden

IJsselmeer

G
E
R
M
A
N
Y

N

km
0 4 8 12 16 20 km

109

WATERWAY	MAP	FROM	TO	KM LONG	No. of LOCKS	LOCK SIZE	DRAFT	HEIGHT
Zwarte Water	96	Vollenhoverkanaal	Zwolle	22.0	0		3.30	5.50
Urkervaart	100	Urk	Emmeloord	12.0	1	7.0X40.5	2.40	6.50
Lemstervaart	101	Emmeloord	Lemmer	15.0	1	7.0X39.0	2.80	6.50
Creilervaart	101a	Lemstervaart	Creil	7.0	0		2.20	4.80
Ruttense Vaart	101b	Lemstervaart	Rutten	5.0	0		2.50	4.80
Zwolse Vaart	102	Emmeloord	Vollenhove	13.0	2	7.0X39.0	2.80	6.50
Enservaart	102a	Zwolse Vaart	Ens	9.0	0		2.00	2.60
Nagelervaart	102b	Urkervaart	Nagele	6.0	0		1.60	5.00
Espelervaart	102c	Emmeloord	Espel	8.0	0		2.00	2.60
Luttelgeestervaart	102d	Zwolse Vaart	Luttelgeest	5.0	0		1.30	3.10
Kadoeler Meer/Zwanendiep	103	Zwarte Meer	Vollenhove	7.0	0		2.80	BB2.6
Vollenhoverkanaal	103a	Vollenhove	Blokzijl	5.0	1	6.8X39.0	1.60	BB2.8
Noorderdiep/Valse Trog	103b	Blokzijl	Giethoornse Meer	3.0	0		1.70	open
Arembergergracht	104	Zwartsluis	Beulaker Wijde	8.0	1	4.45X27.8	1.40	BB3.5
Walengracht	104a	Beuelaker Wijde	Giethoornse Meer	4.0	0		1.60	open
De Riete/Wetering/Heuvengracht/ Kalenbergergracht	105	Giethoornse Meer	Ossenzijl	13.0	0		1.40	5.40
Steenwijkerdiep	105a	Muggenbeet	Steenwijk	8.0	0		1.60	BB
Kanaal Beukers-Steenwijk	106	Meppelerdiep	Steenwijk	15.0	1	7.8X65.0	2.40	BB2.1
Meppelerdiep	107	Zwartsluis	Meppel	10.0	0		3.50	open
Hoogenveense Vaart	108	Meppelerdiep	Hoogeveen	29.0	3	7.5X65.0	2.90	5.30
Verlengde Hoogenveense Vaart	108a	Hoogeveen	Klazienaveen	30.0	2	6.0X40.0	2.50	5.20
Stieltjeskanaal	108b	Veenord	Coevorden	6.0	1	7.5X65.0	2.00	5.90
Oranjekanaal/Bladderwijk	109	Klazienaveen	Emmen	4.0	1	6.0X42.1	2.20	4.20
Drentsche Hoofdvaart	110	Meppel	Assen	42.0	6	6.0X27.5	1.50	5.40
Knl. Steenwijk-Ossenzijl	111	Steenwijk	Ossenzijl	13.0	0		1.80	6.50

WATERWAY	MAP	FROM	TO	KM LONG	No. of LOCKS	LOCK SIZE	DRAFT	HEIGHT
Linde (river)	112	Ossenzijl	Driewegsluis	6.0	1	8.0X60	1.80	BB
Linde (river)	112a	Ossenzijl	Kuinre	9.0	1	5.3X30.0	1.00	2.60
Mallegat	112b	Driewegsluis	Oldemarkt	2.0	0		1.60	open
Linde (river)	112c	Driewegsluis	Blessebrug	7.0	0		1.10	2.50
Nieuwe Kanaal/Tusschen Linde	112d	Kuinre	Schoterzijl	4.0	0		1.10	2.75
Jonkers of Helomavaart	113	Driewegsluis	Kuinder of Tjonger	7.0	0		2.20	BB
De Kuinder of Tjonger	114	Schoterzijl	Pier Christiansloot	5.0	0		1.10	2.95
De Kuinder of Tjonger	114a	De Driesprong	Engelen-vaart	8.0	0		2.40	20.00
Tjongerkanaal	114b	Engelen-vaart	Oosterwolde	25.0	3	5.45X29.0	1.70	3.20
Schipsloot	114c	Kuinder of Tjonger	Wolvega	5.0	0		1.30	2.10
Pier Christiansloot	115	De Driesprong	Tjeukemeer	3.0	0		2.20	BB
Broeresleat of Fjopuwerhuster Feart	115a	Kuinder of Tjonger	Tjeukemeer	3.0	0		2.50	2.40
Waldsleat//Hjerringsleat/Riensleat	116	Sloten	Prinses Margriet Kanaal	3.0	0		1.60	open
Follegasloot	116a	Tjeukemeer	Prinses Margriet Kanaal	3.0	0		2.20	BB
Scharster of Nieuwe Rijn	117	Tjeukemeer	Langweerder Wielen	7.0	0		2.20	BB
Engelen-vaart	118	Tjongerkanaal	Heerenveen	5.0	0		1.80	BB
Heerenveense Kanaal/Het Deel	118a	Heerenveen	Meinesloot/Akkrum	11.0	0		1.80	5.50
Heeresloot/Monnikerak	118b	Heerenveen	Turfroute/Heerenveense	6.0	0		1.70	2.60
Opsterlandse Compagnonsvaart (Turfroute)	119	Heeresloot	Drentse Hoofdvaart	49.0	8	5.5X29	1.50	3.70
Prinses Margriet Kanaal	120	Lemmer	Stroobos	65.0	1	16.0X260	4.20	BB
Lange Sloot/Slotergat	121	Lemmer	Slotermeer	6.0	0		2.00	BB
De Luts/Van Swinderen/Spoekhoekster	121a	Slotermeer	Aldkarre Meer	10.0	0		0.80	2.30
Ee	121b	Slotermeer	Woudsend	0.5	0		1.70	BB2.4
Nauwe Wijmerts	121c	Woudsend	Heeg	1.0	0		2.25	open
Johan Frisokanaal	122	Stavoren	Prinses Margriet Kanaal	27.0	1	9.0X60	2.80	BB
Kruisvaart/Jan Broerskanaal	122a	Johan Frisokanaal	Koudum	2.0	0		1.50	3.00

WATERWAY	MAP	FROM	TO	KM LONG	No. of LOCKS	LOCK SIZE	DRAFT	HEIGHT
Het Var/Koudumer Far	122b	Koudum	Zwarte Woude/Fluessen	2.0	0		1.50	2.10
Woudsender Rakken	122c	Heegermeer	Woudsend	2.0	0		2.00	open
Wellesloot	122d	Woudsend	Prinses Margriet Kanaal	3.0	0		1.80	1.70
Workum Kanaal/Het Zool	123	IJsselmeer	Workum	4.0	1	7.3X35	1.70	BB
Workum Kanaal/Lange Vliet/Korte Vliet	123a	Workum	Gaastmeer	4.0	0		1.70	BB1.2
Workum Kanaal/Inthiemasloot	123b	Gaastmeer	Fluessen	1.0	0		1.70	open
Workumertrekvaart	124	Workum	Bolsward	8.0	0		1.70	BB
Van Panhuijskanaal	125	Makkum	Workumertrekvaart	6.0	0		1.70	BB
Makkumervaart	125a	Makkum	Bolsward	4.0	0		1.20	BB
Bolswarderzijlvaart/De Wijmerts	126	Bolsward	IJlst	8.0	0		2.00	BB
Wijde Wijmerts	126a	IJlst	Heeg	3.0	0		2.00	BB
Geeuw	127	IJlst	Sneek	4.0	0		2.10	BB
Woudvaart	127a	Sneek	Prinses Margriet Kanaal	3.0	0		1.60	4.50
Houkesloot	128	Sneek	Sneekermeer	4.0	0		3.10	open
Meinesloot	128a	Sneekermeer	Akkrum	3.0	0		3.00	BB
Boorne	128b	Akkrum	Turfroute	6.0	0		1.70	BB
Birstumer-Zijlroede	128c	Akkrum	Grou	5.0	0		2.00	BB
Sneekertrekvaart	129	Sneek	Leeuwaarden	20.0	0		1.80	2.50
Franekervaart	130	Sneek	Franaker	24.0	0		1.80	1.60
Bolswardertrekvaart	131	Bolsward	Van Harinxma Kanaal	20.0	0		1.60	2.50
Harlingervaart	132	Bolsward	Harlingen	14.0	0		1.50	2.30
Witmarsumervaart/Arumervaart	132a	Bolsward	Arum	6.0	0		1.50	2.50
Arumervaart	132b	Arum	Franaker	4.0	0		1.00	2.10
Van Harinxma Kanaal	133	Harlingen	Prinses Margriet Kanaal	38.0	0		2.60	BB
Lang Deel/Wartenster wijd	133a	Leeuwaarden	Warten	7.0	0		1.90	BB
Wargastervaart	133b	Grou	Leeuwaarden	8.0	0		1.40	BB

WATERWAY	MAP	FROM	TO	KM LONG	No.of LOCKS	LOCK SIZE	DRAFT	HEIGHT
Dokkumer Ee	134	Leeuwaarden	Dokkum	22.0	0		1.90	BB
Hallumertrekvaart	134a	Dokkumer Ee	Hallum	6.0	0		1.70	2.50
Holwerdervaart	134b	Dokkumer Ee	Holwerd	7.0	0		1.50	2.30
Dokkumer Grootdiep	135	Dokkum	Dokkumer Nieuwe Zijlen	11.0	0		1.90	BB
Nieuwe Vaart/Dokkumer Diep	136	Bergumer Meer	Lauwersmeer	20.0	1	9.0X65	4.00	3.00
De Lits	136a	Bergumer Meer	De Leijen	1.0	0		1.40	BB
Peinder Kanaal	136b	De Leijen	Drachten	5.0	0		1.70	3.20
Stroobossertrekvaart	137	Dokkum	Stroobos	17.0	0		1.00	2.90
Lauwers Zildiep	138	Stroobos	Zoutkamp	12.0	0		1.50	2.60
Reitdiep	139	Lauwersmeer	Groningen	31.0	0		1.70	BB
Van Starkenborghkanaal	140	Stroobos	Groningen	27.0	2	16.0X190	3.50	6.60
Hoendiep/Eendrachtskanaal	141	Zuidhorn	Groningen	9.0	0		1.60	2.10
Aduarderdiep	142	Aduard	Reitdiep	9.0	0		2.00	3.10
Boterdiep	143	Groningen	Uithuizen	14.0	0		1.50	2.90
Winsumerdiep	144	Reitdiep	Westerwijtewerd	8.0	1	6.5X40	1.40	2.60
Westerwijterwerdermaar	144a	Winsumerdiep	Damsterdiep	4.0	1	5.0X28	1.40	2.20
Damsterdiep	145	Eemskanaal/Groningen	Delfzijl	23.0	1	6.0X25	1.60	2.50
Eemskanaal	146	Groningen	Delfzijl	25.0	0		5.00	BB
Termunterzijl Kanaal	147	Delfzijl	Termunterzijl	9.0	1	6.5X25	1.80	BB
Termunterzijl Diep	148	Termunterzijl	Scheemda	9.0	1	6.0X25	1.20	2.50
Slochterdiep	149	Eemskanaal/Groningen	Slochter	6.0	1	6.0X28	1.00	BB
Winschoterdiep	150	Groningen	Westerwoldse Aa	38.0	0		3.50	BB
Westerwoldse Aa	151	Winschoterdiep	Dollard	12.0	2	5.8X40	2.50	BB
Westerwoldse Aa	151a	Winschoterdiep	Wedderveer	6.0	0		2.00	2.50

113

WATERWAY	MAP	FROM	TO	KM LONG	No. of LOCKS	LOCK SIZE	DRAFT	HEIGHT
BL Tijdenskanaal	152	Nieuweschans	Ruiten Aakanaal	9.0	1	6.0X20	1.40	2.50
Ruiten Aakanaal	152a	BL Tijdenskanaal	Ter Apel	9.0	2	6.0X20	1.40	3.00
Pekel Aa	153	Winschoterdiep	Oude Pekala	6.0	0		1.20	BB
Pekel Hoofdiep	154	Oude Pekala	Stadskanaal	16.0	5	5.9X28	1.30	5.00
AG Wildervanckkanaal	155	Winschoterdiep	Veendam	7.0	0		3.00	4.50
Oosterdiep	156	Veendam	Stadskanaal	7.0	3	5.9X38	1.50	BB
Stadskanaal	157	Oosterdiep	Stadskanaal	7.0	3	6.0X38	1.20	5.00
Musselkanaal	157a	Stadskanaal	Ter Apelkanaal	5.0	3	6.0X38	1.20	5.00
Ter Apelkanaal	157b	Musselkanaal	Ter Apel	6.0	0		1.20	BB
Rutenbrockkanaal	158	Ter Apel	Rutenbrock DE	2.0	2	6.0X28	1.50	BB
Drentsche Diep	159	Winschoterdiep	Zuidlaren	6.0	0		2.10	3.00
Noord-Willemskanaal	160	Groningen	Assen	28.0	3	7.5X65	1.90	5.40
Prince Willem Alexander Kanaal (Veenvaart/Veenparkkanaal)	161	Erica	Ter Apel	30.0	4	4.8X28	1.50	3.50

Region D: Yacht Rental Locations

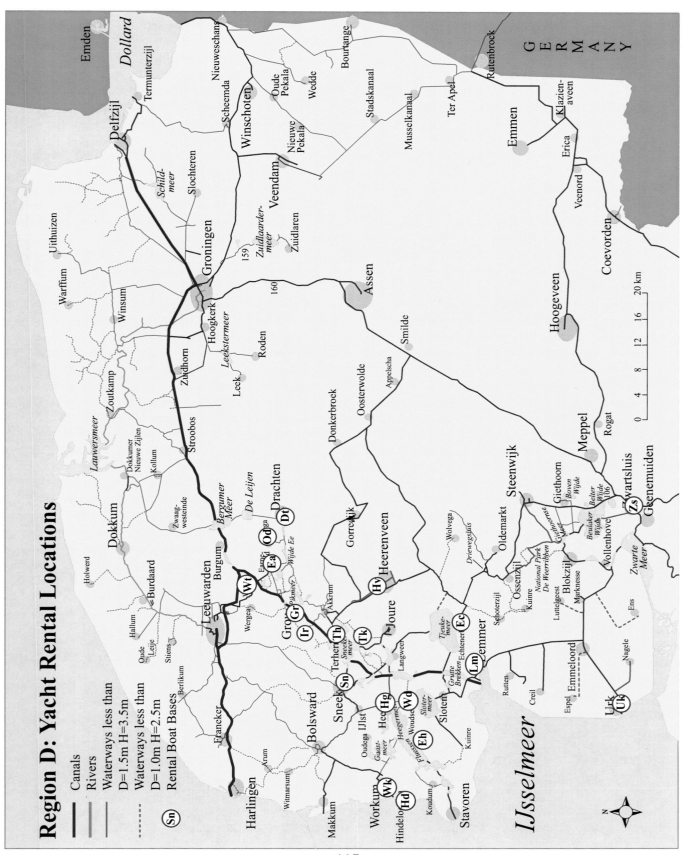

Canals
Rivers
Waterways less than
D=1.5m H=3.5m
Waterways less than
D=1.0m H=2.5m
(Sn) Rental Boat Bases

Map Index Town	Name	Website	Telephone +31(0)	Charter Motor	Charter Sail	Day Motor	Day Sail
Dt Drachten	De Drait	www.dedrait.nl	0512 51 32 76	X		X	
Ea Earnewald	Hoekstra Jachtcharter	www.hoekstra-jachtcharter.nl	0511 53 92 92	X		X	
Ea Earnewald	Yachtcharter Westerdijk	westerdijk.com	0511 53 93 00	X			
Ea Earnewald	Wester Watersport	www.bootverhuurwester.nl	0511 53 92 43			X	
Ec Echtenerbrug	De Driesprong	www.driesprong.net	0561 48 14 73	X			
Ec Echtenerbrug	Yachts4U	www.yachts4u.nl	0561 48 08 08	X			
Ec Echtenerbrug	Turfskip	www.turfskip.com	0514 54 14 67	X		X	
Eh Elahuizen	Allemandsend	www.allemandsend.nl	0514 60 40 80				X
Gr Grou	Hofstra	www.hhofstra.nl	0631 96 02 38	X			
Gr Grou	Anja	www.wsbanja.nl	0566 62 13 73	X		X	X
Hg Heeg	Ottenhome Heeg	www.ottenhomeheeg.nl	0515 44 28 98	X	X	X	X
Hg Heeg	Varskip	www.varskip.com	0515 44 32 67		X		
Hg Heeg	Heech by de Mar	www.heechbydemar.nl	0515 44 27 50		X		
Hg Heeg	Hoora	www.hoora.nl	0515 44 27 15	X		X	X
Hg Heeg	Van Roeden	vanroedenwatersport.nl	0515 44 33 30			X	
Hg Heeg	JFT Watersport	www.jft-watersport.nl	0515 44 38 67		X	X	X
Hv Heerenveen	Bootverhuur Kalf	www.bootverhuurkalf.nl	0634 30 38 85	X			
Hv Heerenveen	Watermerk Yachtcharter	watermerk.nl	0647 08 46 66	X			
Hv Heerenveen	YachtCharter 2000	yachtcharter2000.nl	0653 59 58 78	X			
Hd Hindeloopen	Le Boat	www.leboat.com	0102 13 03 52	X			
Ir Irnsum	Aqualux	www.aqualux.nl	0613 23 93 02	X			
Ir Irnsum	FNMA	www.yacht-charter-holland.eu	0515 33 50 26	X			

Town	Name	Website	Telephone	Charter Motor	Charter Sail	Day Motor	Day Sail
Lm Lemmer	De Brekken	www.brekken.nl	0514 56 21 15	X			
Lm Lemmer	Tacozijl	www.tacozijl.com	0514 56 20 03	X		X	
Od Oudega	Bootsma	www.jachtwerfbootsma.nl	0515 46 99 60			X	X
Sn Sneek	Aquanaut	www.aquanaut.nl	0515 41 22 53	X			
Sn Sneek	Centerpoint	www.centerpoint.nl	0515 42 66 42	X		X	
Sn Sneek	Het Toppunt	www.hettoppunt.nl	0515 42 08 08	X	X	X	X
Sn Sneek	Holiday Boatin	www.holidayboatin.nl	0515 41 37 81	X			
Sn Sneek	Hospes	www.hospes.nl	0515 41 25 94	X	X		
Sn Sneek	Nautica Yachtcharter	www.nauticayachtcharter.nl	0515 55 93 16	X			
Sn Sneek	Sanzi Yacht Charter	www.sanziyachtcharter.nl	0515 42 16 87	X			
Sn Sneek	Yachtcharter Sneek	www.yachtchartersneek.nl	0515 43 83 83	X			
Sn Sneek	Van Straten	www.yachtcharter-vanstraten.nl	0515 43 81 58	X			
Sn Sneek	Veldman	www.vyc.nl	0515 41 36 72	X			
Sn Sneek	Zijda	www.zijda.nl	0515 43 29 93	X			
Th Terherne	Wetterwille	www.wetterwille.nl	0566 68 88 12	X			
Th Terherne	De Schiffart	www.schiffart-yachtcharter.nl	0566 65 19 20	X			
Tk Terkaple	Maran Yachtcharter	www.maran.nl	0566 68 93 05	X	X		X
Wt Warten	Sytze Heegstra	www.yachtcharterheegstra.nl	0582 55 25 46	X			
Wk Workum	Hotel Gast Inn	www.hotelgastinn.nl	0515 54 16 87	X	X		
Wk Workum	Workum Watersport	workumwatersport.nl	0515 54 17 18	X		X	
Wd Woudsend	Wellekom WS	www.wellekom-watersport.nl	0629 27 30 37		X	X	X
Wd Woudsend	Klompmaker	www.klompmaker.nl	0514 56 44 47	X			
Wd Woudsend	Hibo	www.hibo.nl	0514 59 27 44	X			
Uk Urk	Yacht Charter Urk	www.ycu.nl	0527 68 80 01	X			
Zs Zwartsluis	Panorama	www.charter-panorama.nl	0383 86 71 08	X			

Marrekrite free moorings (a map of the popular places in Friesland)

Marrekrite is a partnership between the province of Friesland and 21 municipalities. They maintain over 3,500 berths at 550 locations in Friesland, available to all visitors at no charge (up to 3 days.)
Locations are shown on the map: ● Single mooring area ■ Multiple mooring areas
Go to: www.marrekrite.frl View or download the online map; click on the sailboat image or "Varen" then look for "kaart" in the upper left of the web page.
There is always a container nearby at the moorings. From June to September you can encounter the Marrekrite sewage boat on the Frisian waters, a boat with equipment into which "dirty-water" tanks of pleasure boats can be drained on the spot. This service is free: Phone: 06-10 35 75 02

Friesland

Friesland is primarily a watersports area, although there are many charming amd picturesque cities, towns and villages. The Frisian lake area includes more than 11,000 hectares of water divided between lakes, channels, rivers, canals and pools. But Friesland also has woods and beaches and the Frisian Wadden Islands. All of this in a region 100 km west-east by 80 km north-south, about twice the size of the Heart of Holland, with 65 navigable waterways, more than in the entire country of Germany.

Friesland is the common name for the entire region, however it includes portions of the provinces of Groningen, Drenthe, OverIJssel and Flevoland.

Language and signage used on charts, streets and highways are commonly in both Dutch and Frisian. As in other parts of the country, English is almost always available. But especially in Friesland many visitors are German, therefore a Deutsch option is frequently offered on websites. There are local dialects spoken in some areas. Cultural areas, based on geographical features, are *de Kleistreek*, the clay region along the northwestern coast, *de Friese Wouden,* the Frisian forests in the northeast of the province, and *de Zuidwesthoek*, the southwestern corner.

Other than tourism and watersports services, the primary industry of the region is agricultural.

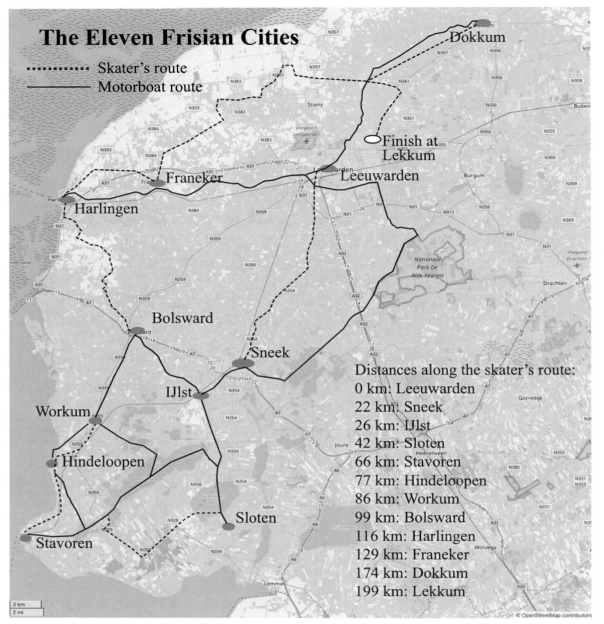

The Eleven Frisian Cities

········· Skater's route
———— Motorboat route

Dokkum

Finish at Lekkum

Franeker

Leeuwarden

Harlingen

Bolsward

Sneek

IJlst

Workum

Hindeloopen

Sloten

Stavoren

Distances along the skater's route:
0 km: Leeuwarden
22 km: Sneek
26 km: IJlst
42 km: Sloten
66 km: Stavoren
77 km: Hindeloopen
86 km: Workum
99 km: Bolsward
116 km: Harlingen
129 km: Franeker
174 km: Dokkum
199 km: Lekkum

3 km
2 mi

© OpenStreetMap contributors

The 11 cities of Friesland encompass the history of the region, with old forts, castles, and ramparts still recognizable today. Stavoren was said to be founded as early as 313 BC, while Harlingen was founded in the 9th century by Vikings. Bolsward is a typical Frisian country town. Sloten is the smallest, with less than 800 inhabitants. A tour route including these cities is a good way to experience the history of Friesland.

The *Elfstedentocht* (Journey of Eleven Cities) is a speed skating competition and leisure skating tour held irregularly. The tour is conducted on frozen canals, rivers and lakes. It is not held every year (last in 1997) because not every Dutch winter permits skating on natural ice. About 15,000 amateur skaters take part. Depth or fixed-bridge clearance along some of the waterways used by the skaters are not sufficient for motorboats. Allow at least one week for a quick tour and two to three weeks for extended visits in the towns.

Elfstedentocht Tour: Harlingen - Franeker - Leeuwarden - Dokkum - Sneek - Sloten

WATERWAY Names are as shown on ANWB charts	FROM	TO	KM	LOCKS	BRIDGES to open	DEPTH minimum	WIDTH locks/ bridges	HEIGHT fixed bridges	TRAVEL TIME hours
Van Harinxma Kanaal	Harlingen	Franeker	8.8	1	3	2.75	12.0	none	
Van Harinxma Kanaal	Franeker	Leeuwarden	15.0	0	3	2.75	12.0	none	
Harlinger Vaart	Van Harinxma Kanaal	Westerstads Gracht	2.4	0	3	3.0	8.0	none	
Harlingen to Leeuwarden			26.2	1	9	2.75	8.0	none	3.5
Westerstads/ Noorderstads Gracht	Leeuwarden	Leeuwarden	1.3	0	2	2.1	8.0	none	
Dokkumer Ie	Leeuwarden	Dokkum	21.7	0	6	1.95	8.0	none	
Leeuwarden to Dokkum			23.0	0	8	1.95	8.0	none	3.0
Van Harinxma Kanaal	Swettehaven, Leeuwarden	Langdeel	6.1	0	3	2.75	12.0	none	
Langdeel	Van Harinxma Kanaal	Wartenster Wiid	2.8	0	0	1.9	open	none	
Wartenster Wiid	Langdeel	Prinses Margriet Kanaal	4.0	0	2	1.9	7.4	none	
Prinses Margriet Kanaal	Wartenster Wiid	Sneekermeer	15.3	0	0	3.2	12.0	7.15	
Sneekermeer	Prinses Margriet Kanaal	Houkesleat	3.8	0	0	4.2	open	none	
Houkesleat	Sneekermeer	Sneek	4.2	0	0	2.75	open	none	
Leeuwarden to Sneek			36.2	0	2	1.9	7.4	7.15	5.0
De Geau (Geeuw)	Waterpoort, Sneek	IJlst	3.5	0	1	1.95	9.0	none	
Wijd-draai	IJlst	Nijezijl	1.0	0	0	2.2	open	none	
Wijde Wijmerts	Nijezijl	Heeg	4.7	0	1	2.2	10.1	none	
Nauwe Wimerts	Heeg	Woudsend	2.9	0	1	1.95	8.0	none	
De Ie	Woudsend	Slotermeer	1.2	0	0	1.7	open	none	
Slotermeer			3.0	0	0	2.0	open	none	
Slotergat	Slotermeer	Sloten	1.6	0	1	1.7	8.0	none	
Sneek to Sloten			17.9	0	4	1.7	8.0	none	2.0

Harlingen - Friesland's port on the Wadden Zee/North Sea

Harlingen is such a thorough boating city that the "Main Street" is a marina, the Noorderhaven. A stroll around this harbor is a must, as is a visit to the Grote Kerk, a church in the southeastern corner of the old city, to view the unusual organ and pulpit.

Visiting boats can enter at sea level from the IJsselmeer through a normally-open lock and pass through Prins Hendrikbrug to tie up on the southern quay just inside the bridge. The Havenkantoor, harbormaster's office, with toilet facilities, is located on that quay at Noorderhaven 34.

Or turn south on the Zuiderhaven for moorings managed by the municipality.

At the eastern end of the Noorderhaven the Leeuwenbrug (above) gives access to the city's canals and the inland waterways. See another photo of the Noorderhaven on page 11, a view looking east.

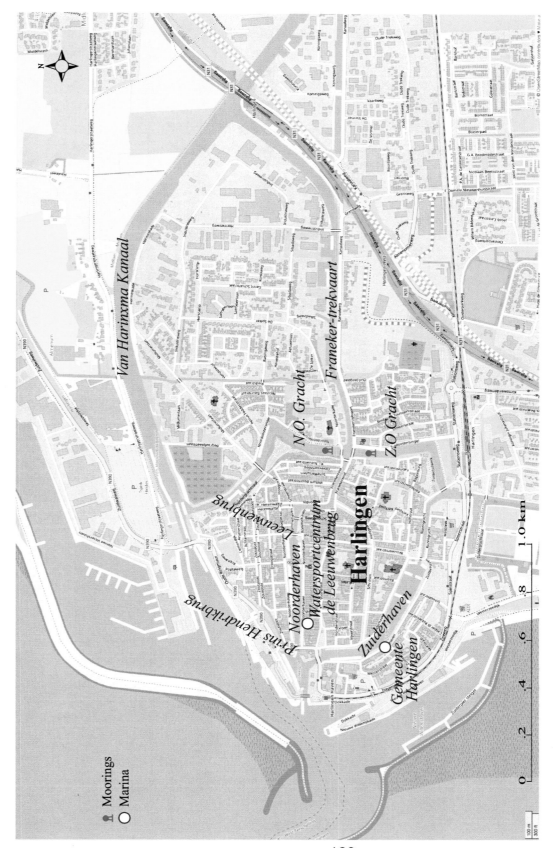

The Van Harinxma Kanaal separates the city from the large and busy commercial port on the northern side; leisure boats arriving from the east should use Franeker-trekvaart into the city center. There are free moorings on the canals N.O. Gracht & Z.O Gracht. at the intersection with Franeker-trekvaart.

Noorderhaven/Zuiderhaven: Marina De Leeuwehbrug

jachthavenleeuwenbrug.nl   0517 41 56 66 / 06 53 84 67 34

Franeker is the home of the oldest working planetarium in the world. An accurately-moving model of the solar system was built between 1774 and 1781. The Planetarium shows the position of the planets, moving around the sun. The planetarium runs through an impressive gear mechanism of wooden hoops and discs with ten thousand hand-forged nails as teeth. A pendulum clock and nine weights drive this whole contraption. The museum also holds an extensive collection of historic astronomical instruments. Also visit the cozy Planetariumcafé. www.planetarium-friesland.nl

Moorings are on the south
of the city at
Gemeente Franekeradeel
www.franekeradeel.nl
06 22 20 95 05

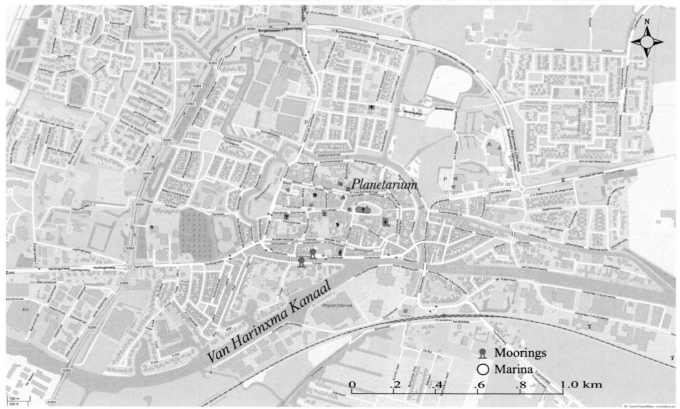

Dokkum is at the end of an extended leg of the Elfstedentocht; skaters cross the strip of sea clay countryside along the coast, roughly west and north of Leeuwarden, to the turning point (Keerpunt) at the bridge shown below and then return to the finish at Lekkum.

The stunning town, best viewed from the water, is located at the edge of the Frisian forests. It retains most of its ramparts and old character. The centre is a very well preserved, large star-shaped fortification which is bifurcated by a central canal. Two of the star bastions have large windmills built on top of them.

There are over 300 mooring places around the town. They all have spectacular views and, despite the number available, it might still be hard to find a spot in the peak of the season.

Gemeente Noardeast Fryslan
www.noardeast-fryslan.nl
0519 29 44 45

125

Leeuwarden is the largest city and the economic hub of Friesland. The Elfstedentocht starts at the Swettehaven, in the southwestern corner of the city and finishes northeast of Leeuwarden, on the Bonkevaart canal, close to the windmill De Bullemolen, near the village of Lekkum.

Built as a star fort, the walls around Leeuwarden no longer exist but the singel (canal moat) still surrounds the city with six prominent star points, making an excellent tour route by boat, cycle or on foot.

The very pleasant *Nooderplantage* and *Prinsentuin* parks fill the three western star points (left & below.) Moorings are available along the twisting path of the waterway through these parks, the *Westerstads Gracht* and *Noorder-stads Gracht*.

Gemeente Leeuwarden
www.leeuwarden.nl 14-058

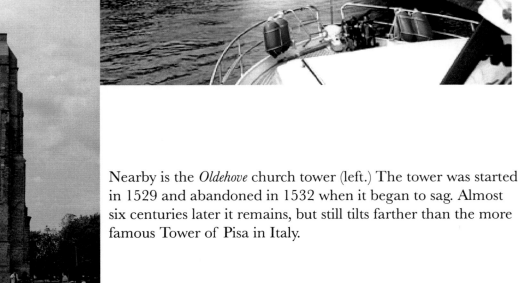

Nearby is the *Oldehove* church tower (left.) The tower was started in 1529 and abandoned in 1532 when it began to sag. Almost six centuries later it remains, but still tilts farther than the more famous Tower of Pisa in Italy.

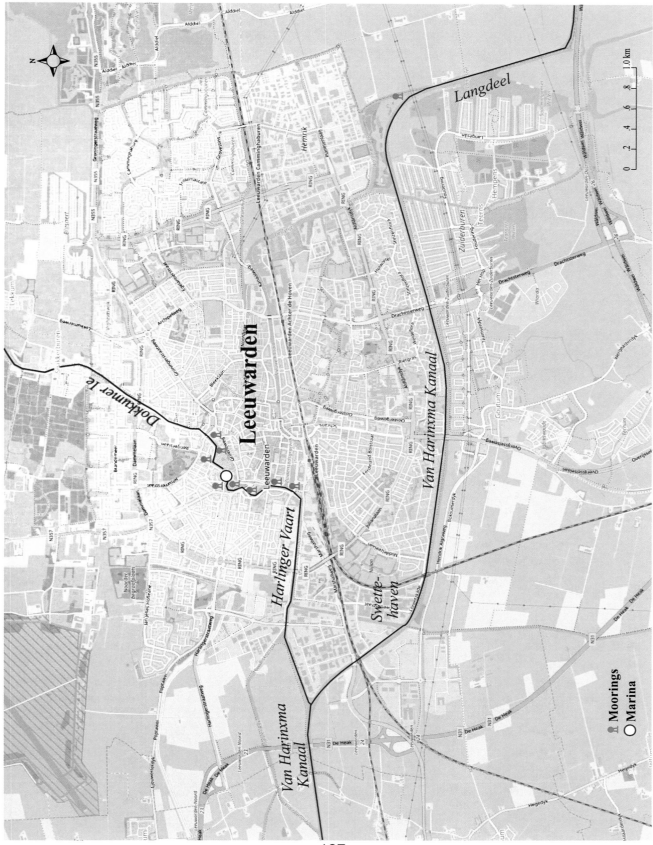

Langdeel

Leeuwarden

Leeuwarden

Dokkumer Ie

Harlinger Vaart

Van Harinxma Kanaal

Van Harinxma Kanaal

Swette-haven

Hemrik

Zuiderburen

Teerns

Goutum

Hempens

⚓ Moorings
◯ Marina

Sneek was the first walled city in Friesland; construction of a moat and wall around the city began in 1492. The notable feature remaining is the *Waterpoort* (below left) at the southwestern corner of the old city. The brick Watertoren faces that gate (right.)

Today Sneek is the boating center of Friesland, not only because it is at the intersection of many waterways and near the lakes, but also because it is the home of many boat brokers, boat builders, charter boat bases and all types of boat services. Sneekermeer is a large group of lakes east of Sneek; several islands offer mooring pontoons and anchoring is common.

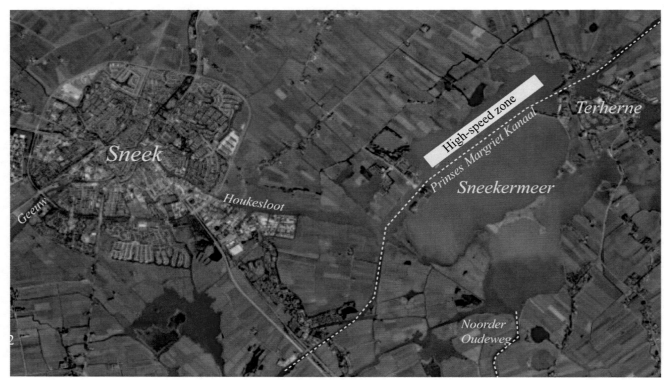

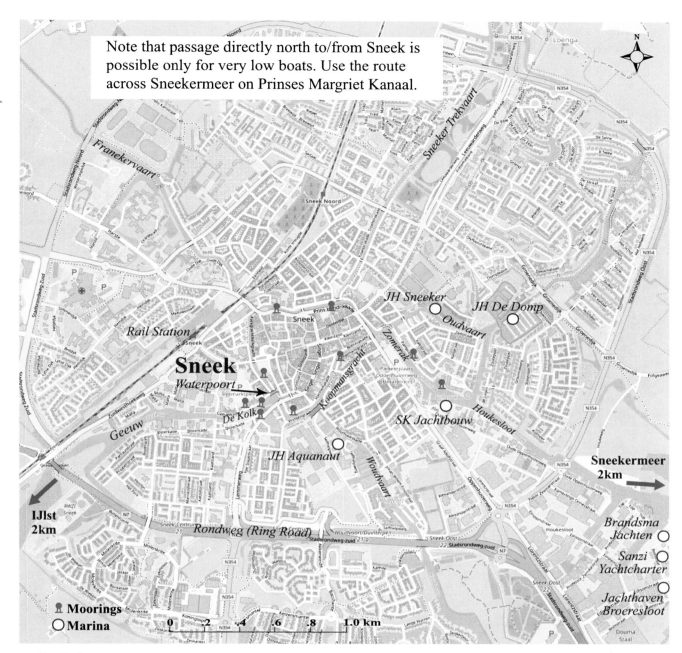

Note that passage directly north to/from Sneek is possible only for very low boats. Use the route across Sneekermeer on Prinses Margriet Kanaal.

Jachthavens
Gemeente Sudwest-Fryslan www.gemeentesudwestfryslan.nl 06 21 94 11 00
B.V. Sneeker Jachthaven www.sneekerjachthaven.nl   06 15 40 98 58
Jachthaven De Domp   www.dedomp.nl/en   0515 75 56 40
Jachthaven Broeresloot   www.broeresloot.nl   0515 75 57 51
Boat Builders
JH Aquanaut Yachting www.aquanaut.nl   0515 43 84 22
Brandsma Yachts   www.brandsmajachten.nl   0515 42 50 00
SK Jachtbouw www.sk-jachtbouw.nl   0515 41 80 50
Yacht Charter
Sanzi Yacht Charter www.sanziyachtcharter.nl   0515 42 16 87

IJlst retains some of its historical buildings and offers a display of beautiful houses with waterfront gardens and a row of pleasant cafes near the central bridge. The view below is seen on arrival from Sneek, just after passing by the windmill De Rat (at right below); it is less than an hour from Sneek, a good choice for a brunch stop. Moorings along the quay at right, near the VVV (tourist) office.

The Passantenhaven (note sign above right) is on a side canal with fixed bridge clearance of 2.3m.
Passantenhaven IJlst 0515 53 18 18

Or stop on the quay at **Woudsend** (left), another hour along the route. The town is very busy with boats in season.

Sloten is the smallest of the 11 towns. The size and basic shape of the town has not changed significantly for hundreds of years. It was originally built with star fortifications on a diamond-shaped moat. Unlike the other towns, this modern town still sits more or less entirely inside the fortifications, in the open landscape with suburbs only at the east and west.

The picturesque canal (below) which runs N/S through the middle of town is lined by old houses displaying the full range of traditional Dutch gables. (Visitors cannot moor on this canal; height is less than 2m.) There are plenty of moorings, many with electricity and other services, on the approaches to the north and south and on the northeastern side of the moat surrounding the town.

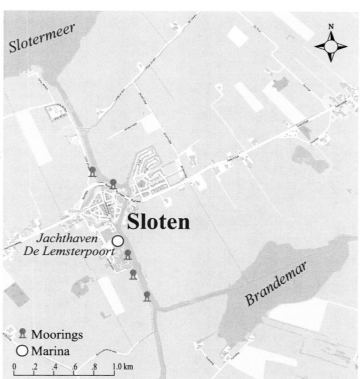

A large marina is at the bottom point of the diamond, near the windmill *De Kaai* (right.)
Jachthaven De Lemsterpoort
www.lemsterpoort.nl
0514 53 16 68

131

Elfstedentocht Tour: Sloten - Stavoren - Hindeloopen - Workum - Bolsward - Sneek

WATERWAY Names are as shown on ANWB charts	FROM	TO	KM	LOCKS	BRIDGES to open	DEPTH minimum	WIDTH locks/bridges	HEIGHT fixed bridges	TRAVEL TIME hours
Slotergat/Slotermeer/De Ie	Sloten	Woudsend	5.8	0	2	1.7	8.0	none	
Waldseinster Rakken	Woudsend	Heeger Meer	2.1	0	0	1.7	open	none	
Heeger Meer			3.7	0	0	2.0	open	none	
De Fluezen (Fluessen)			6.5	0	0	3.0	open	none	
Nije Feart			0.5	0	0	3.0	open	none	
De Oarden			1.2	0	0	3.0	open	none	
De Morra			3.2	0	0	2.8	open	none	
Johan Friso Kanaal	De Geau	Stavoren	5.1	0	1	3.0	9.0	none	
Sloten to Stavoren			28.1	0	14	2.4	9.0	none	4.0
Johan Friso Kanaal	Stavoren	De Morra	5.1	0	1	3.0	9.0	none	
De Morra			1.0	0	0	2.8	open	none	
Jan Broerskanaal	De Morra	Koudumer Far	2.5	0	0	1.7	8.0	3.0	
Yndyk	Koudumer Far	Hindeloopen	4.2	0	0	1.5	6.0	2.57	
Stavoren to Hindeloopen			12.8	0	1	1.5	6.0	2.57	2.0
IJsselmeer	Hindeloopen	It Soal (Het Zool)	2.4	1	0	2.0	open	none	
It Soal (Het Zool)	IJsselmeer	Workum	3.8	1	4	2.0	7.3	none	
Hindeloopen to Workum			6.2	2	4	2.0	7.3	none	2.0
Workumer Trekvaart	Workum	Bolsward	10.3	0	5	1.65	6.8	none	
Workum to Bolsward			10.3	0	5	1.65	6.8	none	2.0
De Wimerts	Bolsward	Nijezijl	9.0	0	5	1.95	7.0	none	
Wijd-draai	Nijezijl	IJlst	1.0	0	0	2.2	open	none	
De Geau (Geeuw)	IJlst	Waterpoort, Sneek	3.5	0	1	1.95	9.0	none	
Bolsward to Sneek			13.5	0	6	1.95	7.0	none	3.0

Stavoren retains the same basic layout as shown in this 1664 map, however none of the original buildings or fortifications remain. It is the western-most point of Friesland on the IJsselmeer (or Zuyder Zee, as noted on the map.) The town boasts a sand beach on the IJsselmeer, six marina complexes and more boats than people!
Moorings at the south end of the island: Gemeente Sudwest-Fryslan 0623 34 78 25 VHF 74

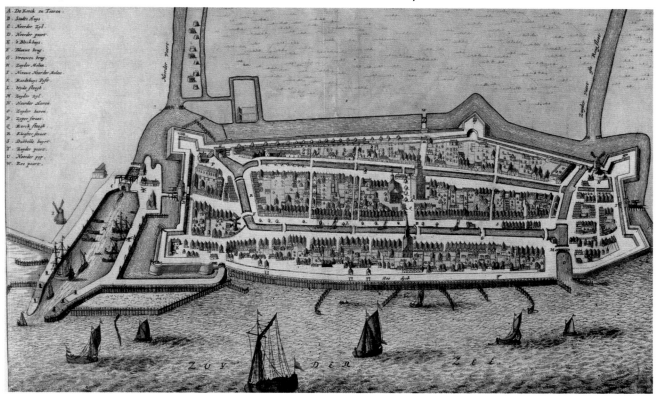

Hindeloopen is a small port on the IJsselmeer. Wander through the narrow streets to view the wooden bridges and buildings with characteristic Dutch façades. At the museum you can learn about the town's rich maritime history, another small museum is devoted to the Elfstedentocht.

Alongside the lock into the old harbor, the Sylhús (lock keepers house, left) is a national monument. Nearby, majestic St Gertrude's church dominates a point of land stretching into the IJsselmeer; the interior of the church is simple yet beautiful.

Moorings can be found in the center of town south of the handsome wooden footbridge (height 2.57m.)
Jachthaven Hindeloopen
www.jachthavenhindeloopen.nl
0880 50 41 57

Workum is located three kilometers from the IJsselmeer, accessed via Het Zool canal. The town is split down the middle by the Djippe Dolte (Deep Dolte); the old town center is on the west side. St Gertrude's church, the major building, has a free-standing tower (right.) Many residences and shops are national monuments, part of the protected historical village. Seventeen windmills can be found in the immediate vicinity.

Within the town there are six commercial marinas and many quay-side moorings, as well as a new municipal harbour (gemeentehaven) in a basin just off west side of the main canal.

Gemeente Sudwest-Fryslan 06 53 20 40 34

Jachthaven It Soal www.itsoal.nl 0515 54 29 37

JH Bouwsma www.watersportwinkeldeliefde.nl 0515 54 20 04

DeHaan Watersport www.dehaanwatersport.nl 0515 54 17 97

Workum Watersport www.workumwatersport.nl 0515 54 17 28

Heida Jacht en Motorenservice www.heidaworkum.nl
0515 54 18 55

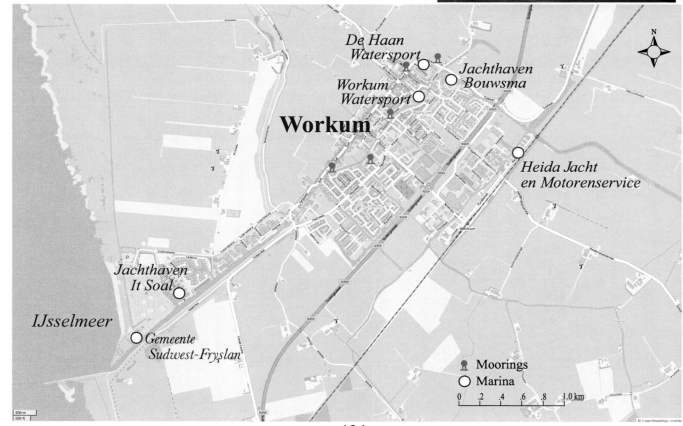

Bolsward welcomes visiting boaters at the Stoombootkade (steamboatquay, below) adjoining the Grootzand canal, which leads into the center of the old town. Interior canals are navigable only by dinghy. The singel (perimeter canal) is navigable but restricted on the east side by bridges as low as 1.2m; west side bridges are bascule bridges. Moorings on the south and west sides.

Gemeente Sudwest-Fryslan www.gemeentesudwestfryslan.nl 0651 57 99 15

The major building to view in Bolsward is not a church, rather it is the City Hall (right) which features a bell, a clock and a carillon in its tall spire. It is located on the Appelmarkt, the main shopping street, which runs east-west through the middle of the town, straddling the central canal.

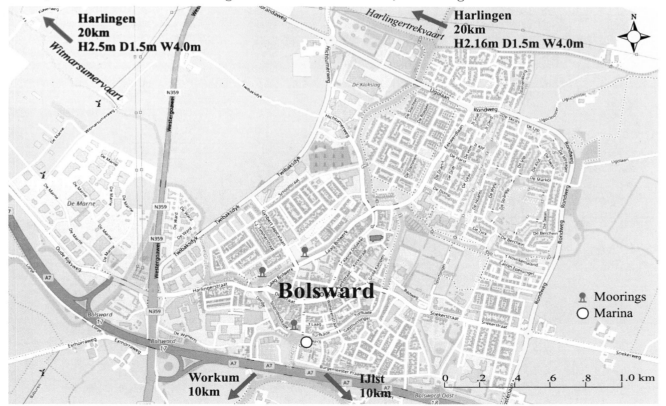

Harlingen 20km H2.5m D1.5m W4.0m

Harlingen 20km H2.16m D1.5m W4.0m

Bolsward

Moorings
Marina

Workum 10km

IJlst 10km

0 .2 .4 .6 .8 1.0 km

Friesland - Red Tour

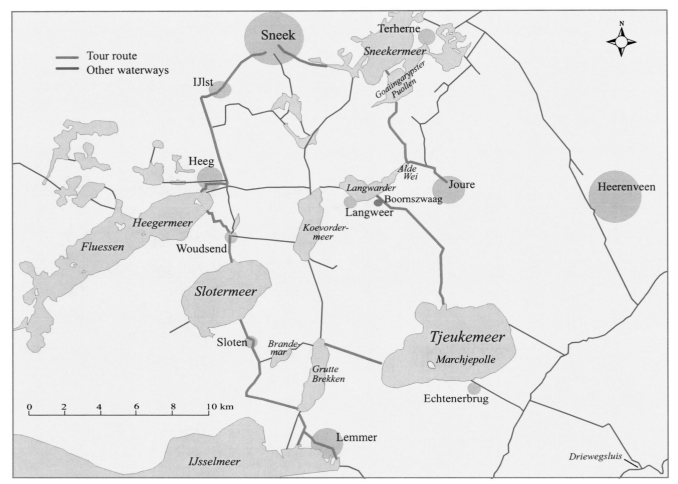

The lakes of Friesland are explored in this tour, which begins at Sneek. Each day's travel time is short, allowing more time to enjoy the waters, beaches and islands of these lakes.

Day 1 - Leave Sneek (see pages 128-129) for the Sneekermeer; the day could be spent traveling through the adjoining lakes, then on to a stop at the town of Joure.

Day 2 - Return to the Langwarder and visit the town of Langweer before traveling south to the Tjeukemeer for an island mooring at Marchjepolle.

Day 3 - Go west to Prinses Margriet Kanaal and follow that busy waterway into the town Lemmer, on the IJsselmeer.

Day 4 - The charming town of Sloten is the next overnight stop, in the center of open fields (page 132).

Day 5 - Leave Sloten and travel north through the busy intersection at Woudsend and then on to Heeg, a sailing capital.

Day 6 - Return to Sneek with a stop for lunch in IJlst (see page130).

Red Tour: Sneek - Joure - Tjeukemeer - Lemmer - Sloten - Heeg - IJlst - Sneek

WATERWAY Names are as shown on ANWB charts	FROM	TO	KM	LOCKS	BRIDGES to open	DEPTH minimum	WIDTH locks/ bridges	HEIGHT fixed bridges	TRAVEL TIME hours
Simmerrak/Houkesleat	Sneek	Sneekermeer	5.8	0	0	2.75	open	none	
Sijbesloot	Sneekermeer	Goaiingarypster Puollen	1.7	0	0	1.8	open	none	
Noarder Alde Wei	Goaiingarypster Puollen	Alde Wei	3.4	0	0	1.7	open	none	
Jouster Sylroede	Alde Wei	Joure	1.7	1	0	2.0	6.9	none	
Sneek to Joure			12.6	1	0	1.7	6.9	none	2.0
Jouster Sylroede	Joure	Alde Wei	1.7	1	0	2.0	6.9	none	
Langwarder Wielen	Jouster Sylroede	Boornzwaag	2.2	0	1	1.5	8.0	11.5	
Skarster Rien	Boornzwaag	Tjeukemeer	7.5	0	2	1.9	6.9	none	
Joure to Tjeukemeer			11.4	1	3	1.5	6.9	11.5	2.0
Follegasloot	Tjeukemeer	Grutte Brekken	5.4	0	1	1.9	8.0	12.0	
Grutte Brekken	Follegasloot	Prinses Margriet Kanaal	3.8	0	0	1.5	open	none	
Stroomkanaal	Grutte Brekken	Lemmer	2.0	0	0	2.15	open	none	
Tjeukemeer to Lemmer			11.2	0	1	1.5	8.0	12.0	2.0
Stroomkanaal	Lemmer	Grutte Brekken	2.0	0	0	2.15	open	none	
Langesloot	Grutte Brekken	Tacozijl	2.7	0	1	2.0	6.98	none	
Ie of Boomsvaart	Tacozijl	Sloten	2.8	0	0	2.0	open	none	
Lemmer to Sloten			7.5	0	1	2.0	7.0	none	1.5
Slotergat/Slotermeer/De Ie	Sloten	Woudsend	5.8	0	2	1.7	8.0	none	
Waldseinster Rakken	Woudsend	Heeger Meer	2.1	0	0	1.7	open	none	
Sloten to Heeg			7.9	0	2	1.7	8.0	none	2.0
Wijde Wijmerts	Heeg	Nijezijl	4.7	0	1	2.2	10.1	none	
Wijd-draai	Nijezijl	IJlst	1.0	0	0	2.2	open	none	
De Geau (Geeuw)	IJlst	Waterpoort, Sneek	3.5	0	1	1.95	9.0	none	
Heeg to Sneek			9.2	0	2	1.95	9.0	11.5	
Total Red Tour			59.8	2	9	1.5	6.9		9.5

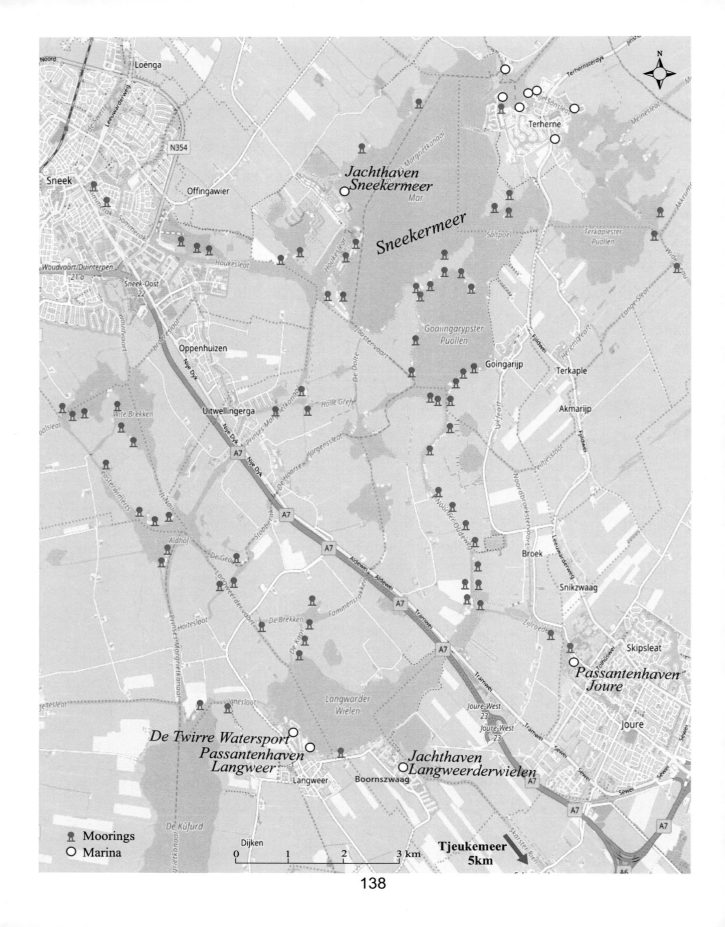

Friesland - Red Tour

Sneekermeer is a large lake with many moorings (and many boats, in season.) There are seven marinas in and around Terherne (see page 156) as well as:

Jachthaven Waterrijck Sneekermeer www.sneekemeer.nl 06 34 38 71 16

Joure is a very pleasant village, now grown into a town by residential waterfront developments on the outskirts. It is popular with summer boating visitors, but there always seems to be room for one more. Visit the clock/barometer shop and the museum in the town center. There are several restaurants. A special treat for boaters is a tour of the De Jong boatworks, builder of beautiful wooden Frisian vessels.

Passantenhaven www.passantenhaven-joure.nl 06 22 05 25 12

Gemeente De Fryske Marren www.defryskemarren 14-0514

Jachtwerf De Jong www.jachtwerfdejong.nl 0513 41 26 64

Langweer is a classic Dutch town, a great place to walk around town, cycle along the small canals or relax on the sandy beach adjacent to the Oude Haven. The Passantenhaven, with 300 spaces, is especially friendly and comfortable. The lake is a sailing center with many events during the summer; day rental of sailboats is available.

Passantenhaven Langweer www.passantenhavenlangweer.nl 06 27 62 65 28

Service, Sailboat rentals: De Twirre Watersport www.twirre.nl 0513 49 90 10

Boornszwaag: Jachthaven Langweerderwielen www.jachthavenlangweerderwielen.nl
06 24 52 14 18

Tjeukemeer - Lemmer - Sloten - Woudsend

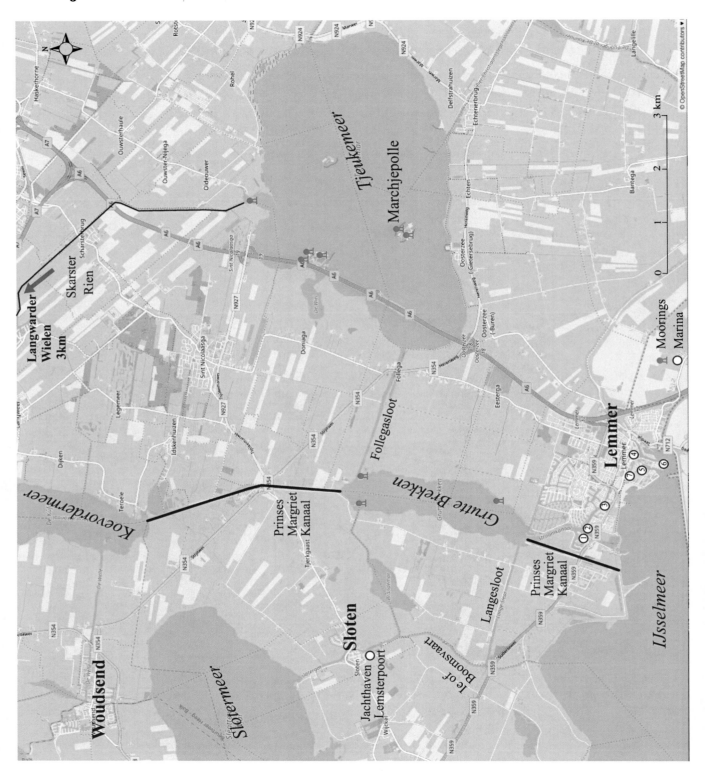

Lemmer is an important harbor for Friesland; most vessels arriving from the IJsselmeer will come here to enter the canals. It is at the western end of the cross-Friesland Prinses Margriet Kanaal and also offers easy access to many of the lakes of the region. There are many choices of municipal moorings or marinas, used by both canal travelers and IJsselmeer sailors. Canalside moorings may be available in the center of town along the Zijlroede, beyond the bridge shown in the photo; as can be seen, however, this is a popular and busy area.

Lemmer binnenhaven (inner harbor)
...everywhere you look there are just boats and more boats. It is a great place to just sit and watch the antics of others sailors. The town is well served by shops and restaurants and a beach so is busy in the height of summer...

(See map on page 140)

1. Watersportcentrum Tacozijl tacozijl.nl   06514 56 20 03
2. Jachthaven Iselmar   www.iselmar.nl   06 53 43 70 63
3. Binnenjachthaven   www.lemmerbinnen.nl   0514 56 19 79
4. Jachthaven Lemster Baai   lemsterbaai.nl   06 15 24 65 64
5. Jachthaven De Punt   www.jachthavendepunt.nl   06 29 33 18 04
6. Jachthaven Friese Hoek Lemmer   www.friesehoek.nl   0880 50 41 32
7. Jachthaven De Boei   www.boatcity.nl   06 53 83 11 03

Woudsend and **Heeg** are probably the most thoroughly saturated towns in Friesland in terms of recreational boating. They are centrally located in the Friese meren, the largest area of lakes in the region; each town has canals pointing north, east, south and west for easy access to the nearby Slotermeer and Heegermeer or on for visits to other towns. Both towns offer a large range of boating services, including the availability of day or weeklong charter of sailboats, modern or traditional.

The town quay at Woudsend is classic Dutch, from the church at the north end to the windmill on the south.

Heeg (left) is a sea of marinas and the waterways that connect them.

Woudsend (see map next page):

1. Jachthaven/camping: Recreatie Centrum De Rakken www.derakken.nl   0514 59 15 25

2. Jachthaven Schraa Watersport www.schraawatersport.nl   0514 59 17 76

3. Chandler/jachthaven/sailboatbuilder: De Welle www.watersportbedrijfdewelle.nl   0514 59 13 03

4. Jachthaven/sailboat charter: Wellekom Watersport www.wellekom-watersport.nl   0514 59 28 00

5. Chandler/accessories: Karibu Yachting www.karibu.nl   0514 59 23 55

6. Jachthaven Reekers Watersportbedrijf www.reekerswatersport.nl   0514 59 20 18
    Boatbuilder/service of custom sailing yachts: Breehorn BV www.breehorn.nl   0514 59 22 33

7. Charter of motor yachts: Jachtcharter Klompmaker www.klompmaker.nl   0514 56 44 47

8. Boatbuilder/service of custom motoryachts: Bootwerk BV www.bootwerk.nl   0514 59 17 11

9. Service of engines: Technisch Watersportbedrijf Kooij www.kooijwatersport.nl   06 53 70 31 57

10. Service: Dragt Yachtservice VOF   0514 59 19 70

Heeg is certainly the sailboat center of Holland. There are hundreds of sailboats based here, both privately owned and for charter, by day or week. There are scores of one-design sailboats which compete in races on the Heegermeer. Fleets of *platbodem* traditional sailing barges are available for charter. Motor cruisers may feel a little out of place but are welcome at the Passantenhaven or one of several marinas; there is a Grand Banks dealer here to raise the motoring flag.

1. Passantenhaven Heegerwal   www.heegerwal.nl   06 22 41 61 65 / 0515 44 37 53
2. Jachthaven Eendracht www.jachthaveneendracht.nl 0515 44 25 75
   Boatyard: Jachtwerf Piersma www.windenwater.nl   06 10 28 08 82
3. Charter: Hoora Verhuur www.hoora.nl   0515 44 27 15
4. Jachthaven Gouden Bodem www.vanroedenwatersport.nl   0515 44 33 30
5. Waypoint Heeg jachthaven   0515 44 33 38
6. Jachthaven Heech bij de Mar BVwww.heechbydemar.nl   0515 44 27 50
7. Jachthaven/platbodem charter/broker Varskip   www.varskip.com   0515 44 27 55
   Grand Banks motoryacht dealer: Kremer Nautic www.kremernautic.nl   0515 44 29 66
8. Jachtwerf Heeg www.jachtwerf-heeg.nl   0515 44 22 37
9. Jachthaven/charter/broker Ottenhome Heeg www.ottenhomeheeg.nl   0515 44 28 98

Fuel: Fa. Kooistra en Kuiper   0515 44 24 62
Service, woodwork: VOF Scheepsbetimmering J. H. Pronk   0515 53 17 66
Service, engines: Eeuwe de Jong Scheepsmotoren www.scheepsmotoreneeuwedjong.nl 0515 44 35 43
Stentec Software Heeg www.stentec.com   0515 44 35 15
Centerpoint Charters www.centerpoint.nl   0515 42 66 42

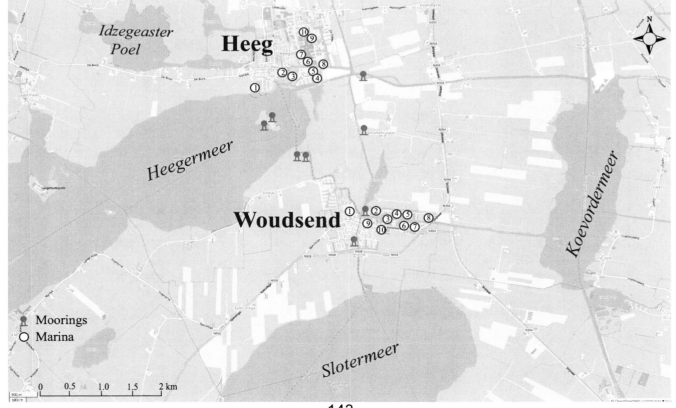

Friesland - Blue Tour

This tour centers on National Park De Weerribben, an extensive wetland area with bogs, swamps, small canals and meadows. Free moorings are available canalside along the waterways De Riete, Wetering, Heuvengracht and Kalenbergergracht. Hundreds of boats use these waterways during the summer months. Canoe routes extend out through the park.

Day 1. The circuit begins at Zwartsluis; travel through northern OverIJssel province to Blokzijl.

Day 2. Enter the national park and select a mooring, perhaps near thevillage of Ossenzijl.

Day 3. Follow the narrow canals to Kuinre and on to Echtenerbrug or the Tjeukemeer.

Day 4. Visit the town of Oldemarkt, via Driewegsluis.

Day 5. View the beautiful homes of Giethoorn by dinghy/tour boat and enjoy one of the restaurants.

Day 6. Return to Zwartsluis via Beulaker Wijde.

Blue Tour: Zwartsluis - Blokzijl - Ossenzijl - Echetenerbrug - Oldemarkt - Giethoorn

WATERWAY Names are as shown on ANWB charts	FROM	TO	KM	LOCKS	BRIDGES to open	DEPTH minimum	WIDTH locks/ bridges	HEIGHT fixed bridges	TRAVEL TIME hours
Zwarte Water	Zwartsluis	Zwarte Meer	6.3	0	0	3.3	open	none	
Kadoeler Meer	Zwarte Meer	Vollenhove	5.6	0	1	3.0	10.4	none	
Vollenhoverkanaal	Vollenhove	Blokzijl	5.3	0	1	2.8	7.0		
Zwartsluis to Blokzijl			17.2	0	2	2.8	7.0	none	2.5
Noorderdiep/Valse Trog	Blokzijl	Giethoornse Meer	3.0	1	1	1.6	6.8	none	
De Riete	Giethoornse Meer	Muggenbeet	1.0	0	1	1.6	6.8	5.4	
Wetering	Muggenbeet	Grote Gat	4.2	0	1	1.4	6.8	none	
Heuvengracht	Grote Gat	Kalenberg	2.2	0	1	1.4	7.3	none	
Kalenbergergracht	Kalenberg	Ossenzijl	4.5	0	0	1.4	open	none	
Blokzijl to Ossenzijl			14.9	1	4	1.4	6.8	5.4	3.0
Ossenzijlersloot	Ossenzijl	Linde river	1.0	0	1	1.8	6.8	none	
Linde	Ossenzijlersloot	Kuinre	8.0	0	0	1.0	5.7	2.6	
Nieuwe Kanaal	Kuinre	Slijkenburg	2.3	0	0	1.15	5.1	2.7	
Tusschen Linde	Slijkenburg	Schoterzijl	2.5	0	0	1.15	5.1	2.7	
De Kuinder of Tsjonger	Schoterzijl	Et Wiede	5.8	0	0	1.1	5.3	3.0	
Pier Christiaansloot	Et Wiede	Echtenerbrug	3.1	0	1	2.25	7.9	none	
Ossenzijl to Echtenerbrug / Tjeukemeer			22.7	0	13	1.65	6.8	5.5	4.0
Pier Christiaansloot	Echtenerbrug	De Kuinder of Tsjonger	3.1	0	1	2.25	7.9	none	
Jonkers of Helomavaart	De Kuinder of Tsjonger	Driewegsluis	6.9	0	2	2.25	7.9	none	
Linde/Mallegat	Driewegsluis	Oldemarkt	3.0	0	0	1.6	open	none	
Echtenerbrug to Oldemarkt			13.0	0	3	1.6	7.9	none	2.5
Linde/Mallegat	Oldemarkt	Driewegsluis	3.0	0	0	1.6	open	none	
Lende (Linde) river	Driewegsluis	Knl Steenwijk-Ossenzijl	3.1	1	0	2.0	open	none	
Ossenzijlersloot	Linde river	Ossenzijl	1.0	0	1	1.8	6.8	none	
Kanaal Steenwijk-Ossenzijl	Ossenzijl	Steenwijk	12.9	0	5	1.8	6.8	none	
Kanaal Beukers-Steenwijk	Steenwijk	Giethoorn	5.2	0	3	2.4	6.8	none	
Oldemarkt to Giethoorn			25.2	1	12	1.8	6.8	none	6.0
Kanaal Beukers-Steenwijk	Giethoorn	Meppelerdiep	9.0	1	2	2.4	5.6	none	
Meppelerdiep	Knl Beukers-Steenwijk	Zwartsluis	3.3	0	0	3.5	open	none	
Giethoorn to Zwartsluis			12.3	1	2	2.4	5.6	none	2.0
Total Blue Tour			105.3	3	34	1.0	5.6	2.6	20.0

OverIJssel Province (northern section)

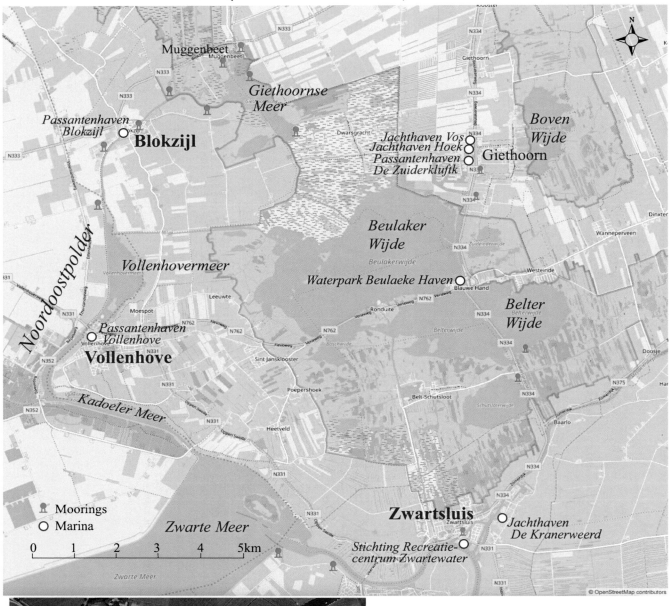

The left side of the map above (west of the north-south channel) is the Noordoostpolder. In earlier times that area was in the open waters of the Zuider Zee. The towns of Vollenhove and Blokzijl (left) were seaports. Flooding was a real danger before the Noordoostpolder and the Afsluitdijk were constructed in the 1930-40's.

Zwartsluis is an historical boating center and an important gateway into the lakes and natural areas of northwestern Overijssel, as well as the inland route into Friesland and Drenthe. Situated at the intersection of the major waterways Zwarte Water and Meppelerdiep, the Arembergergracht also links the town with the Beulaker and Belter lakes as well as the national park and other natural areas to the north. National (historical) Tugboat Days are held here in May of even years. Moorings are available in the center of town. Full services are offered by multiple sources:

     Jachthaven De Kranerweerd www.kranerweerd.nl 0383 86 73 51

     Stichting Recreatiecentrum Zwartewater www.watersportzwartsluis.nl 0383 86 66 52

     Service: PWR Motoren   www.pwrmotoren.com   0383 86 68 69

     Service: Jachtwerf Lok www.jachtwerflok.com 06 53 62 69 99

     Service: Aquaservice www.aquaservice.nl 085 023 95 50

     Charter: Jachtcharter Panorama www.charter-panorama.nl 0383 86 71 08

Vollenhove, "the city of palaces", was once an important harbor on the Zuider Zee, now it is well inland on the eastern edge of the Noordoostpolder. It is worth an extended walking tour past the former palaces and through the many gardens, both formal and natural. Along with the large outer harbor there are limited spaces for small boats along the walls of the Binnenhaven, the old inner harbor. Shops and restaurants are convenient to the moorings.

Jacht en Passantenhaven Vollenhove
www.havensweerribbenwieden.nl
06 20 65 89 79
Service: Jachtwerf Aquador
www.aquador-vollenhove.nl
0527 24 21 12

Blokzijl is a star fort with a very popular boating harbor, surrounded by a charming town with houses dating from the 1600s. Entering the haven through the original flood gates (below) is like stepping back in time.

Original 17th century buildings line the four quays of the haven; the spire of the Grote Kerk rises above the red tile roofs.

If all moorings in the haven are taken or if you just want a more peaceful dock, there is a quay on the west bank of the canal 300 meters south of the floodgates (see page 146.)

Passantenhaven Blokzijl   www.havensweerribbenwieden.nl   06 51 50 83 22

The marshland section of **Nationaal Park De Weerribben**, with navigable canals, stretches north from Muggenbeet. The canalside mooring at right is near Kalenberg, a village offering a restaurant and tavern.   www.pieterjongschaap.nl

Ossenzijl is a small town at the northern edge of the park with a full range of services for visitors. It is a good base for walking through the fens, cycling along the water or paddling a canoe route, with or without a guide. Bird watching among the reeds will show many species. Plenty of free moorings or find full services at:

Jachthaven De Kluft www.dekluft.nl 0561 47 73 70

DSA Yachts   www.vri-jon.nl   0561 47 77 00

JH Ossenzijl www.jachthavenossenzijl.nl
                              0561 47 81 00

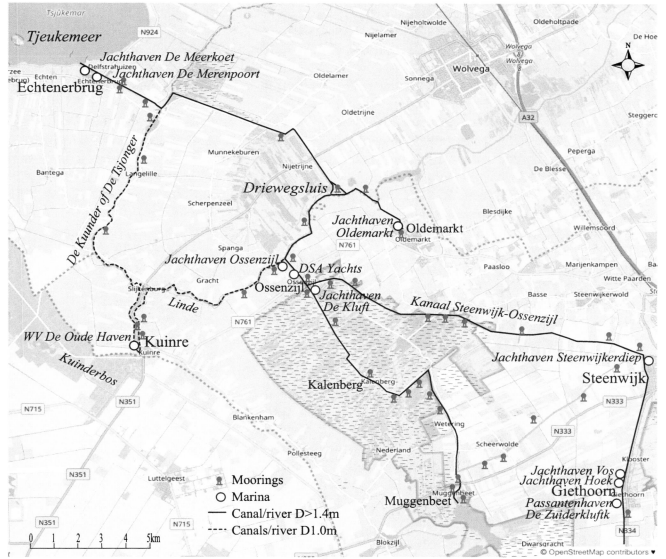

Echtenerbrug is a small but busy town on the major tourist route adjoining the Tjeukemeer.

Jachthaven de Meerkoet
  de-meerkoet.nl
  0514 54 11 01

Jachthaven de Merenpoort
  www.merenpoort.com
  0514 54 14 63

Kuinre is another town which had been a seaport on the Zuider Zee, before the Noordoostpolder was created. Fishermen's houses were built on the land between the two rivers Linde and Kuinder. The death knell for the fishing port came with the reclamation of the Zuiderzee in 1942. The lock which joined the rivers was unused and Kuinre was a forgotten village, wedged between the old and new country. It was renewed by opportunities for water sports in subsequent years. The old lock was excavated and served to connect the Overijsselse lakes and the Frisian lakes. Nearby the *Kuinderbos* (Kuinre forest) offers trails and the remains of a stone forest in a large area of dense woods.
Note that the Linde river has a depth of 1.0 meter, restricting this route to shallow-draft boats.

The **Driewegsluis** (3-way lock) is part of the intersection of the Linde river with the route northwest into Friesland, Jonkers of Helomavaart and Pier Christiaansloot, connecting to the Tjeukemeer.

Although the Driewegsluis has been restored the usual passage is through the Homansluis (at left) and the self-operated Wolvegabrug (at right.) As can be seen, many boats tie up along the islands; the round pavilions offer a restaurant and snacks.

Paviljoen Driewegsluis   www.driewegsluis.nl

Oldemarkt is, as its name implies, a market town from the 1400s. It offers shops and restaurants among its classic buildings. The town lies at the end of the Mallegat, a 1.5km cut from the Linde river. Walk or cycle through a beautiful and centuries old hedgerows landscape on a spur of a moraine. Unique flora and fauna, along with flocks of sheep, are seen on both sides of the paths and roads.

Passantenhaven Oldemarkt havensweerribbenwieden.nl/oldemarkt-3/   06 20 93 90 72

Steenwijk is the major city of the region, a center for shopping and all types of businesses. The rail station here serves routes north to Leeuwaarden and south to Utrecht and Schiphol airport.

Passantenhaven Steenwijk havensweerribbenwieden.nl/steenwijk-3/ 06 22 74 56 22

Jachthaven Steenwijkerdiep www.jachthavensteenwijkerdiep.nl 0521 52 04 00

Giethoorn is the "Green Venice" of the Netherlands; tourists from around the world come here to see the thatched-roof farmhouses, hotels and restaurants from the many tiny canals. Guided tourboats are available or use your own dinghy.

Passantenhaven De Zuiderkluft
havensweerribbenwieden.nl/giethoorn-3/
 06 53 62 40 10

Punterwerf Wildeboer
marina/punt rental/wooden boat builder
www.punterwerf.com
0521 36 12 03

Jachthaven Hoek
www.jachthavenhoek.nl
0521 36 20 22

Jachthaven Vos Giethoorn
www.jachthavenvos.nl
0521 36 21 84

Beulaker Wijde is a large lake south of Giethoorn; it is used by hundreds of small boats. The route south to Zwartsluis is at the eastern side of the lake, through the town of Blauwe Hand.

Waterpark Beulaeke Haven www.waterparkbeulaekehaven.nl 0522-281815

Northern Friesland/Groningen - Ruby Tour

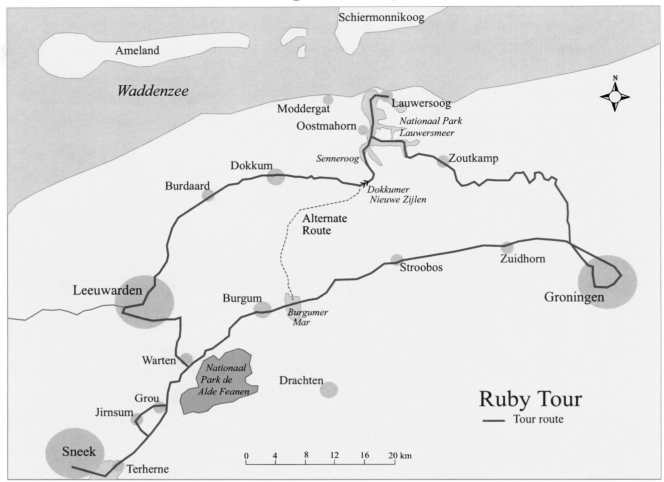

This tour of northern Friesland includes only five days of travel, leaving plenty of time for extended visits in the two national parks, on the Waddenzee or in the interesting towns. And although Groningen is a city well worth a visit, the alternate route removes 56km of travel.

Day 1. From Sneek travel directly to Leeuwarden, or take excursions through Jirnsum and Grou, or spend some time in the National Park de Alde Feanen.

Day 2. A short trip to Dokkum leaves most of the day free to tour the town, or stop for brunch in Burdaard at *Restaurant It Posthûs*, at their terrace on the canal alongside the central bridge.

Day 3. It is a pleasant morning cruise to the National Park Lauwersmeer. Find an isolated stop at an island or go into the town of Lauwersoog.

Day 4. Start early for the 8-hour trip to Groningen; arrive in time for a tour of the city. Or return via the alternate route, skipping a visit to Groningen.

Day 5. Return to Sneek via Prinses Margriet Kanaal.

Ruby Tour: Sneek - Leeuwarden - Dokkum - Lauwersmeer - Groningen - Sneek

WATERWAY Names as shown on ANWB charts	FROM	TO	KM	LOCKS	BRIDGES to open	DEPTH minimum	WIDTH locks/ bridges	HEIGHT fixed bridges	TRAVEL TIME hours
Houkesleat	Passantenhaven, Sneek	Sneekermeer	4.2	0	0	2.75	open	none	
Sneekermeer	Houkesleat	Prinses Margriet Kanaal	3.8	0	0	4.2	open	none	
Prinses Margriet Kanaal	Sneekermeer	Wartenster Wiid	15.3	0	0	3.2	12.0	7.15	
Wartenster Wiid	Prinses Margriet Kanaal	Langdeel	4.0	0	2	1.9	7.4	none	
Langdeel	Wartenster Wiid	Van Harinxma Kanaal	2.8	0	0	1.9	open	none	
Van Harinxma Kanaal	Langdeel	Harlinger Vaart	7.5	0	0	2.75	12.0	5.3	
Harlinger Vaart	Van Harinxma Kanaal	Westerstads Gracht	2.4	0	3	3.0	8.0	none	
Sneek to Leeuwarden			37.6	0	5	1.9	7.4	5.3	5.0
Westerstads/ Noorderstads Gracht	Leeuwarden	Leeuwarden	1.3	0	2	2.1	8.0	none	
Dokkumer Ie	Leeuwarden	Dokkum	21.7	0	6	1.95	8.0	none	
Leeuwarden to Dokkum			23.0	0	8	1.95	8.0	none	3.0
Dokkumer Grutdjip	Dokkum	Dokkumer Nieuwe Zijlen	11.0	0	3	1.95	8.9	none	
Dokkumer Djip	Dokkumer Nieuwe Zijlen	Lauwersmeer	4.0	1	0	2.3	9.0	none	
Lauwersmeer	Senneroog	Lauwersoog	9.8	0	0	2.5	open	none	
Dokkum to Lauwersmeer			24.8	1	3	1.95	8.9	none	3.5
Lauwersmeer	Lauwersoog	Zoutkamperril	9.8	0	0	2.9	open	none	
Zoutkamperril	Lauwersmeer	Zoutkamp	7.5	0	0	2.6	open	none	
Rietdiep	Zoutkamp	Groningen	32.5	3	18	1.7	8.8	none	
Lauwersmeer to Groningen			49.8	3	18	1.7	8.8	none	8.0
Van Starkenborgh Kanaal	Groningen	Stroobos	27.3	2	6	4.0	15.3	6.8	
Prinses Margriet Kanaal	Stroobos	Burgumer Mar	12.9	0	3	3.2	12.0	7.3	
Prinses Margriet Kanaal	Burgumer Mar	Sneekermeer	26.8	0	2	3.2	12.0	none	
Sneekermeer	Prinses Margriet Kanaal	Houkesleat	3.8	0	0	4.2	open	none	
Houkesleat	Sneekermeer	Passantenhaven, Sneek	4.2	0	0	2.75	open	none	
Groningen to Sneek			75.0	0	5	2.75	12.0	7.3	10.0
Total			210.2	4	39	1.7	7.4	5.3	29.5
Alternate route total			153.5	0	0	1.1	6.2	2.95	20.0

Terherne is a seasonal watersports center on the northern edge of the Sneekermeer, with marinas, brokers and yacht charter bases. Terherne Haven is a wharf for classic boats only, with adjacent small cottages for rent. The lock at Terherne on the Prinses Margriet Kanaal stays open.

Jachthaven Sneekerhof www.sneekerhof.nl   0566 68 95 95 / 06 24 72 03 20

Jachthaven Terhernster Syl www.waterrecreatie.com   0566 68 93 51

Jachthaven de Hoorne www.terhernenautic.nl   0566 68 92 64

Terherne Haven www.terhernehaven.nl   0566 65 27 07 / 06 23 37 61 56

Oksewiel Jachthaven www.oksewiel.nl   0566 68 92 77 / 06 16 80 26 44

Jirnsum (Irnsum) is located on the river De Boarn, 4km northeast of Terherne. Here there are more marinas, yacht charter and free moorings.

Jachthaven De Boarnstream www.boarnstream.nl   0566 60 08 28 / 06 83 89 04 00

RFU Jachtspecialist www.rfu-jachtspecialist.nl   0566 60 18 81 / 06 11 36 63 54

Grou is a village not to be missed, if only for lunch and a stroll. Once an isolated fishing village, it is now another of the major boating centers of Friesland. The nearby Pikmeer lake is often filled with sailboats and motorboats of all types.

Gemeente Leeuwarden (passantenhaven) www.leeuwarden.nl   06 53 15 12 98

Watersportbedrijf Anja www.wsbanja.nl   0566 62 13 73

Grouwster Watersport www.grouwsterwatersport.nl   0566 62 31 80

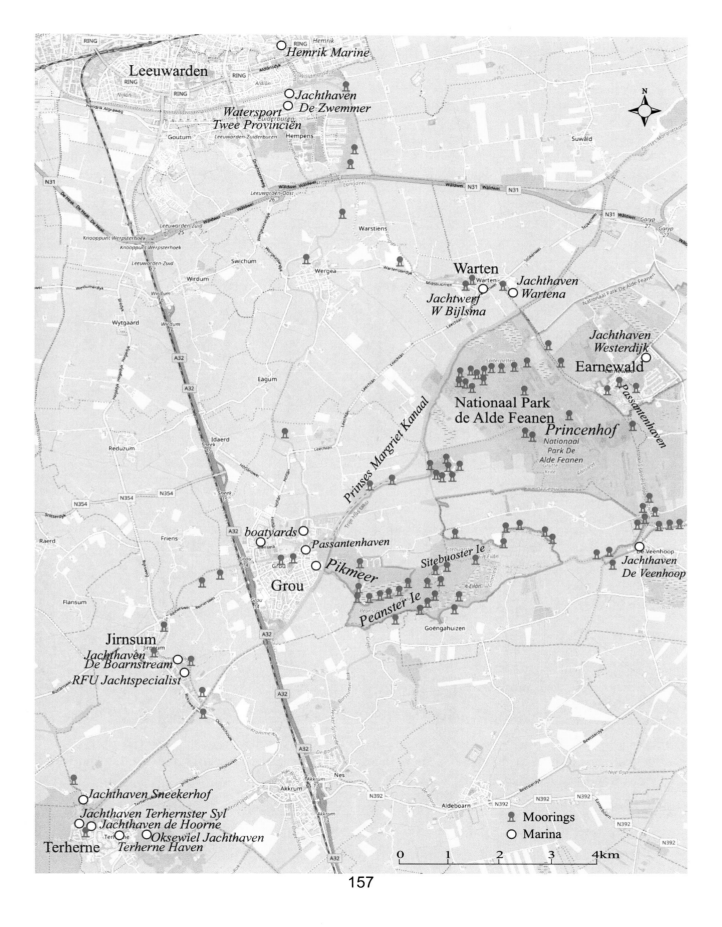

Hemrik Marine

Leeuwarden

Jachthaven
De Zwemmer

Watersport
Twee Provinciën

Goutum
Leeuwarden-Zuiderburen
Hempens

Suwâld

Warstiens

Warten

Jachthaven
Wartena

Jachtwerf
W Bijlsma

Jachthaven
Westerdijk

Earnewald

Swichum
Wergea

Nationaal Park
de Alde Feanen

Princenhof

Wirdum

Passantenhaven

Eagum

Nationaal
Park De
Alde Feanen

Wytgaard

Idaerd

Reduzum

Prinses Margriet Kanaal

Jachthaven
De Veenhoop

boatyards

Passantenhaven

Sitebuoster Ie

Raerd

Friens

Pikmeer

Flansum

Grou

Peanster Ie

Goëngahuizen

Jirnsum

Jachthaven
De Boarnstream

RFU Jachtspecialist

Akkrum

Nes

Aldeboarn

Jachthaven Sneekerhof

Moorings

Jachthaven Terhernster Syl

Marina

Jachthaven de Hoorne

Oksewiel Jachthaven

Terherne

Terherne Haven

0   1   2   3   4km

Princenhof - Alde Feanen National Park: The "Old Fen" is approximately 25 sq km of natural space. Part of the national park is the lake area named Princenhof. The Alde Feanen is a versatile fenland with lakes, peat bogs, ditches, mires, reedbeds, marsh marigold meadows and swamps. In the fields are more than 450 species of plants and more than one hundred bird species. There are nearly fifty marked mooring places, Marrekrite and other free docks, along with many suitable anchorages.

Note: A detailed chart is required to navigate the narrow channels and varying depths of Alde Feanen/Princenhof. Use ANWB chart 1, Friesland, Waterkaarten app or Friese Meren digital chart available from www.stentec.com

Earnewald, a large watersports center, is the only developed area of the park. There are rows of man-made islands and canals built for holiday homes, with water access to every house.

Passantenhaven Earnewald www.havenearnewald.nl 06 12 14 26 31

Jachtcharter Westerdijk   www.westerdijk.com   0511 53 93 00

Jachthaven De Veenhoop www.de-veenhoop.nl 06 46 09 66 10

Warten is a pleasant small village with docks and a choice of excellent waterfront restaurants. East of town is a large marina which welcomes *passanten*; on the west side is a boatyard/marina with covered storage for *winterstalling*.

Stichting Jachthaven Wartena www.jachthavenwartena.nl 0582 55 18 70

Jachtwerf W. Bijlsma www.wbijlsma.nl 0582 55 06 08

Gemeente Leeuwarden (passantenhaven) www.leeuwarden.nl 06 53 80 43 30

*We set off around **Leeuwarden**. The main canal passes south of the town and then we turned right and cut back through the centre of town with some 6 bridges to negotiate at a cost of €6 bruggeld. It is a very picturesque waterway... We moored on the wide grassy bank on the inside of the moat, in a very picturesque setting named the Noorderplantage. These are excellent moorings, with electricity, water and two shower/toilet/wastewater pumpout stations, one at each end of the moorings, accessed via a prepaid card. Boaters moored on the outside can cross the singel on a free foot ferry. The Prinsentuin park separates the quay from the historic city center.*

Gemeente Leeuwarden
www.leeuwarden.nl
14 058

Jachthaven De Zwemmer
www.jachthavendezwemmer.nl
06 51 59 63 10

Watersport Twee Provinciën
watersporttweeprovincien.nl
0582 88 54 46

Hemrik Marine
www.hemrikmarine.nl
0582 88 00 07

Tourist information:
www.visitleeuwarden.com

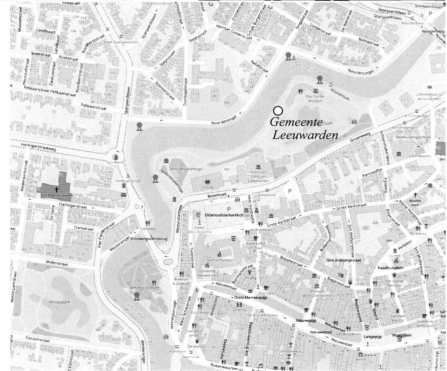

The canal through **Burdaard** forms part of a through route used by both sailing yachts and motor cruisers from Harlingen on the West coast via Leeuwarden and Dokkum to Lauwersoog on the North coast (see Staande Mastroute page 23.) *Restaurant It Posthaus* is on the terrace at the raised bridge.

Passantenhaven Mounehiem (at the molen)   www.burdaard.nl   06 10 85 84 36

Dokkum is a delightful town. It was a fortified town, completely surrounded by a *singel* canal with raised banks. At six points around the outer banks or wall of the town are the remains of what were cannon emplacements.
On two of these have been built large windmills, one of which is shown at right. The town is typically Dutch and a true delight.
See a map of the town on page 125.

Gemeente Noardeast Fryslan
www.noardeast-fryslan.nl
0519 29 44 45

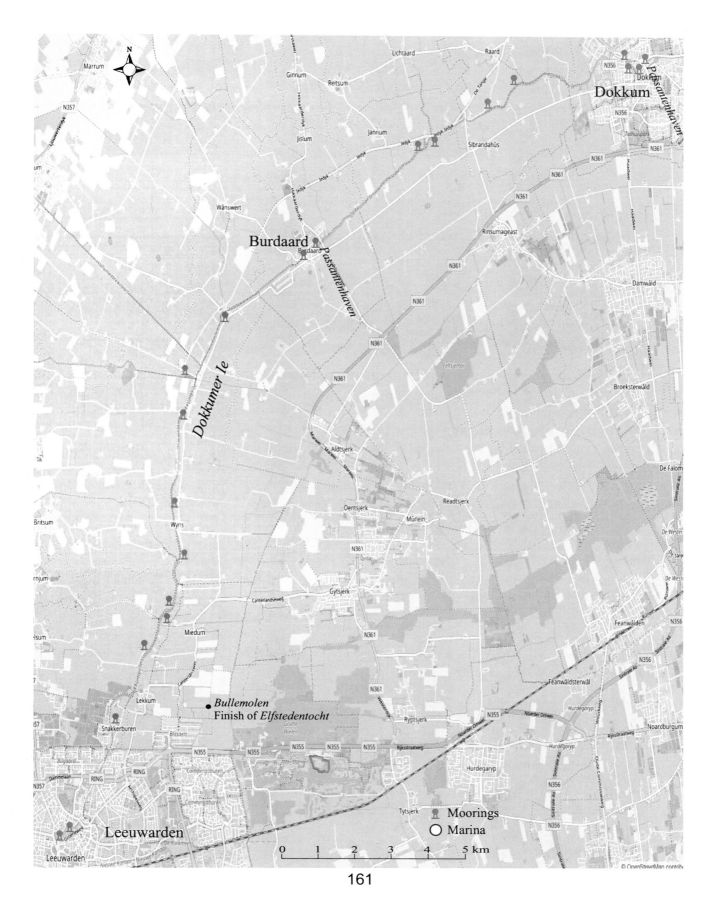

Nationaal Park Lauwersmeer

A Dutch television show *The most beautiful place in the Netherlands* named the Lauwersmeer as third place after the Overijssel nature reserve De Weerribben and the Frisian village Moddergat. As Moddergat is just 5.5km west of the haven at Oostmahorn (by land) this beautiful area holds two honors out of three! (De Weerribben is part of the Blue Tour in this guide.)

East of Dokkum the river is named the Dokkumer Grootdiep, one of the most pleasant cruising rivers in Holland. It is calm, of uniform width, with no islands or obstructions, so it is much like a canal as far as steering the boat goes. But it is much more enjoyable than a straight-line canal. It twists across the wide-open landscape in sweeping curves; eventually the river makes a long series of curves to the south and back again, a section too shallow for some boats. A straight cut connects the northern ends of the loop; at the eastern end of the cut is an important old lock, the *Dokkumer Nieuwe Zijlen*. It was actually "new" in 1729 when the lock and substantial dikes were completed to prevent the sea from flooding into Friesland. At the southern side of that island is the much newer lock and bridge that is the through-passage into the Lauwersmeer and the nature reserve. Four km north boaters can tie-up overnight at the small island near the entrance to the Lauwersmeer. It offers a very sheltered quay, inside a cut across the island. An excursion by dinghy west to the *Senneroog* shore finds a small sandy beach, for wading and swimming. This area is the *Ezumakeeg* nature reserve, a prime location for birdwatchers where there can be seen many species.

> Jachthaven Lunegat   www.lunegat.nl   0511 40 83 03

Halfway up the western side of the Lauwersmeer is the village of Oostmahorn, with a jachthaven and resources for visitors. There is a direct road to Moddergat for travel by bicycle or public bus.

> Jachthaven Lauwersmeer   www.jachthavenlauwersmeer.nl   0511 40 81 00
> Waddeninzicht yacht rental   www.waddeninzicht.com   0519 32 17 12 / 06 22 70 12 44

At the northern end of the Lauwersmeer is the port of Lauwersoog, a fishing village with ferries to Schiermonnikoog, and the Robbengatsluis for passage into the Waddenzee. View: lauersoog.nl

> Jachthaven Lauwersoog   www.noordergat.nl   0519 34 90 40
> Watersportbedrijf R. Jansma   www.rjansma.nl   0519 34 91 10

Depart for Groningen via the Slenk arm of the Lauersmeer. This can be an 8-hour trip; leave the Lauwersoog no later than 08:00 in order to arrive at Groningen before bridge restrictions at 16:00.

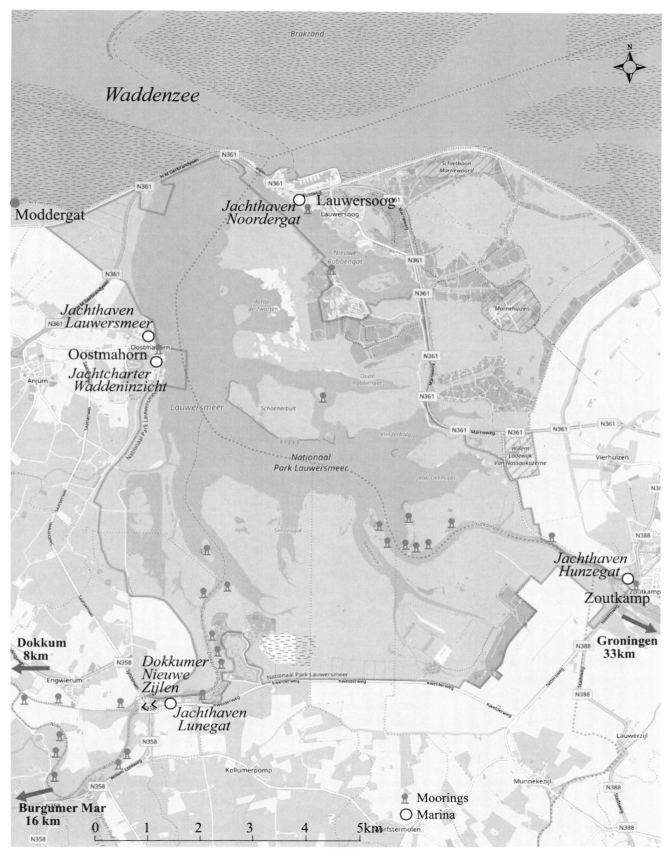

Waddenzee

Brakzand

Moddergat

Jachthaven
Noordergat

Lauwersoog

Jachthaven
Lauwersmeer

Oostmahorn

Jachtcharter
Waddeninzicht

Lauwersmeer

Nationaal
Park Lauwersmeer

Jachthaven
Hunzegat

Zoutkamp

Dokkum
8km

Dokkumer
Nieuwe
Zijlen

Jachthaven
Lunegat

Groningen
33km

Burgumer Mar
16 km

Moorings

Marina

0   1   2   3   4   5km

163

Zoutkamp is a fishing village with at least fifteen seafood restaurants and fish stores, scattered throughout the small town, all within a 1 km walk from the marina or passantenhaven.

Jachthaven Hunzegat   www.hunzegat.nl   0595 40 28 75

Binnehaven Zoutkamp   www.havenzoutkamp.nl   06 12 82 38 84

Follow the Reitdiep river as it twists and turns across the flat plain of far northern Holland. It is a pleasant ride but the waterway is not as scenic as the Dokkumer, the view is one of nonstop fields, with only two bridge crossings and no windmills until De Meeuw, ten miles north of Groningen.

An alternative to the 8-hour cruise from the Lauwersmeer to Groningen on the Reitdiep is to stop overnight about two-thirds along the way and use the extra time to visit the charming, historic mound village of Ezinge by bicycle, a walk or even by dinghy. It is 4.4km from docks at Garnwerd or 3.4km from Aduarderzijl. The 13th-century church with free-standing tower is shown at right.

A good reason to stop at Garnwerd is to allow the 10km approach to Groningen, through 16 opening bridges, two locks and a crossing of the major west-east route Van Starkenborgh Kanaal, to be done in mid-morning rather than at the end of a long day. A very peaceful night could be spent at a small pontoon at the mouth of the Aduarderdiep or at the quay 500m inside the bridge. Somewhat less peaceful but with more facilities is the town of Garnwerd, offering three restaurants and docks with water, toilets, showers and electricity.   Jachthaven Garnwerd aan Zee   www.garnwerdaanzee.nl

06 33 10 53 39

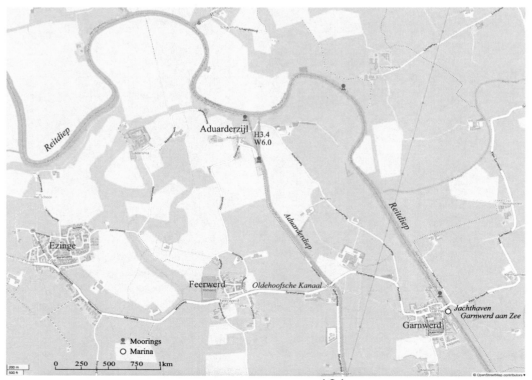

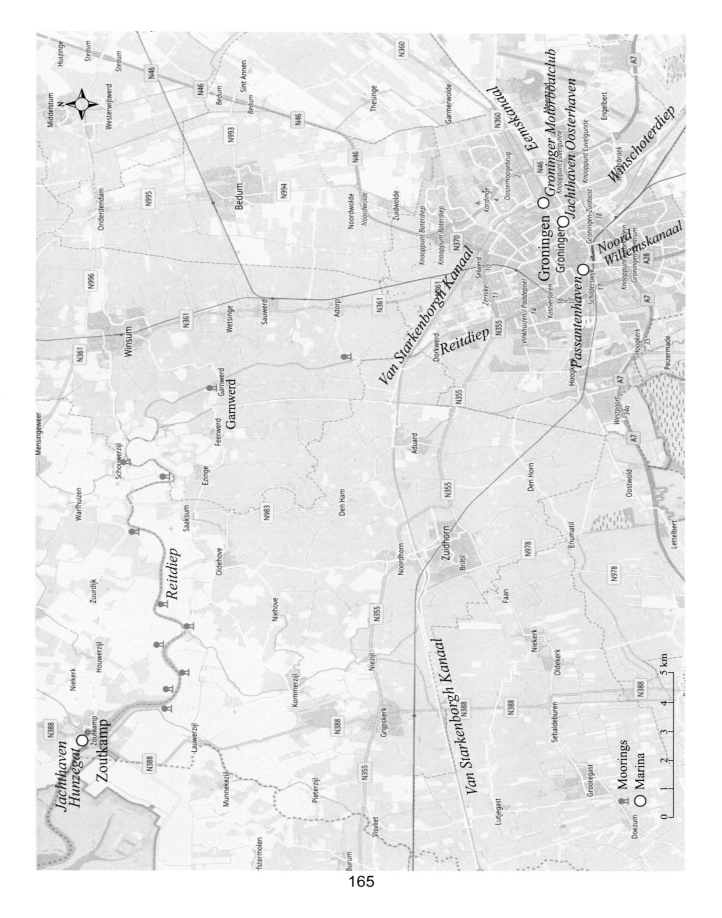

Groningen

The largest city in the north of Holland, it is the provincial capital, with a large university (45,000 students.) The old city is encircled by canals; many magnificent old buildings sit alongside modern office buildings and shops. The main pedestrian street, Herestraat, runs south from the Grote Markt, with most of the city's everyday shopping needs. Other shopping streets extend out from the Grote Markt and the Vismarkt; all streets within the central canal ring are low traffic due to restrictions. The most picturesque shopping street is called the Folkingestraat; it runs south from Korenbeurs (the cornexchange) at the western end of the Vismarkt straight towards the museum bridge and Main Station. It has a lot of little shops full of firsthand and secondhand little gifts, intercultural foods and great books. The historic waterway museum Het Noordelijk Scheepvaartmuseum shows the history of transport over water up through the 1970's.

Arriving southbound on the Rietdiep, the entrance to the star-fort city center is at the Plantsoenbrug, where the canal straight ahead is the Noorderhaven, permanent home of dozens of barges, rafted two or three abreast. That is a sight which would attract any boater, a must-do stroll while in Groningen. (No visitor's moorings.)

The Groninger Museum (at left and below) is the home to various expositions of local, national, and international works of art, most of them modern and abstract. Three radically modernist structures form the museum, along the Verbindingskanaal.

The museum opened in 1994 with the goal of creating more than just a shell for the display of modern art, but to be a work of art itself. The architects have indeed created this, literally an island of modern art, in the middle of a rather mundane city. A pedestrian bridge to the museum leads on across the canal to the main railway station.

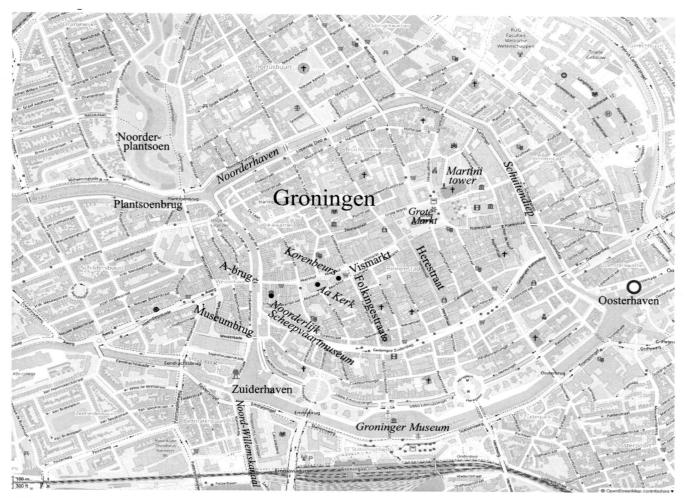

There are two convenient visitor's moorings, within easy walkng distance of all sights and restaurants: on the west the municipal haven is along the quay at Zuiderhaven, with electricity and water. On the east is a full-service marina and watersports shop, the Oosterhaven.

Jachthaven Oosterhaven   www.jachthavenoosterhaven.nl   06 11 34 32 02

At the intersection with the Van Starkenborghkanaal, 1.4km east of the Oosterhaven, there is another full-service marina: Groninger Motorbootclub   www.groningermotorbootclub   050 31 41 728

Groningen is the turn-around point for most cruisers, returning to Sneek via the Prinses Margriet Kanal. But the city is also the hub for other routes:

Northeast on the Eemskanaal to Delfzijl then into East Frisia and northwestern Germany, or along the coast of the North Sea, perhaps to the Baltic Sea through the Kiel Canal.

Southeast on the Winschoterdiep to the German border for visits to the star forts towns of Bourtange and Coevorden.

South on the Noord-Willemskanaal through Drenthe province then further on the IJssel river to southern Netherlands or west on the Turfroute back into Friesland.

The through route across
Friesland from the IJsselmeer
to Groningen is the Prinses
Margriet Kanaal (right) and the
Van Starkenborgh Kanaal
(below.)

Both of these, as well as the
Van Harinxmakanaal from
Harlingen, are broad, straight
waterways heavily
used by commercial traffic.

There is always room for the "little guy", who must keep a sharp watch
and be ready to move out of the main channel.

Turfroute

This is a peaceful series of waterways through a very different Friesland; the canals were created for transport of the extensive peat digging that was carried out here in the 19th century. It is a pristine area in southeastern Friesland enclosed by the Frisian forests.

Traveling through the region is a relaxed and comfortable experience, away from the rush of boats on the Friese lakes during summer. But the skipper and crew are also active, meeting with lock keepers and the local people, and there is plenty to do off the boat - nature, events, bicycling, restaurants and museums.

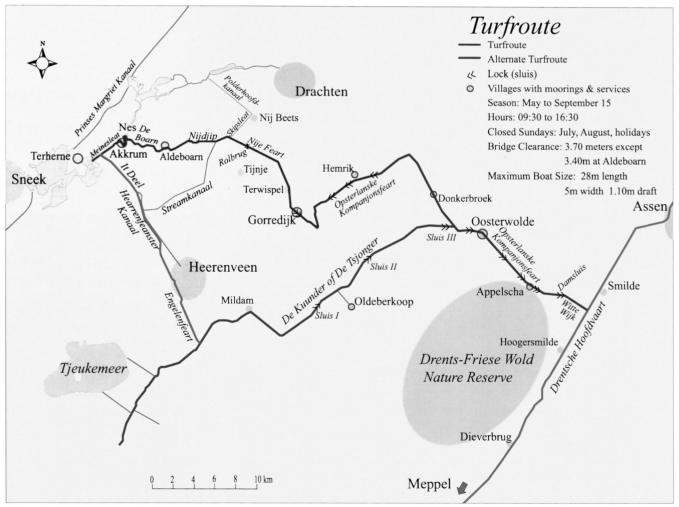

Turfroute

— Turfroute
— Alternate Turfroute
⌁ Lock (sluis)
○ Villages with moorings & services
Season: May to September 15
Hours: 09:30 to 16:30
Closed Sundays: July, August, holidays
Bridge Clearance: 3.70 meters except
3.40m at Aldeboarn
Maximum Boat Size: 28m length
5m width 1.10m draft

Nij Beets features the Sudergemaal pumping-station museum and an open-air museum It Damshûs. The latter gives a good picture of the poor living and working conditions of the peat workers and the excavation of the bogs. www.damshus.nl Moor near the Zuidersluis for a 2km excursion north to Nij Beets or cross the Rolbrug (rolling bridge) to find a beautiful bike path through a nature reserve to the old village of Tijnje.

Gorredijk was an important trading center in the 18th century; it continues as a busy town serving the region of Opsterland. Right in the village is the first and biggest lock of the Turfroute. In the center of the town, near the lock, is a cultural museum displaying the history of peat digging, with numerous artifacts from that period. www.museumopsterlan.nl Two passantenhaven are provided along the south bank: a caravan park at the western end of town with water, electricity, toilets and showers and at the eastern end of town (with no facilities) a wooden dock in a small group of trees or, further along, a brick quay just before the jog in the canal. Either area is a short walk from town center.

After a very pleasant stretch of the Turfroute from Hemrik to Donkerbroek there is a passantenhaven along the east bank at the southern edge of **Donkerbroek** with electricity, water and toilets. From the bridge in the center of the village go one block west to the White House restaurant, where you can find information on the local area. www.restauranthetwittehuis.nl

The **Tsjonger** river joins the canal 3 km south of Donkerbroek and 4 km north of Oosterwolde, at Sluis III. **Oosterwolde** welcomes boaters arriving from the west with a pleasant passantenhaven in a park, however the entrance is under a footbridge with 2.4m clearance. More convenient moorings, with services, are along the north-bank quay between the footbridge and the central road bridge. Most shops are on the south side of the main canal but first walk north to the end of the side canal; in the next block north is Bakkerij Jansen en Terpstra for delicious bread and pastries.

Halfway between Oosterwolde and Appelscha is a little jewel: the restored lock keeper's house at *Fochtelerverlaat* lock. **Appelscha** offers a long wooden quay on the north bank, with facilities, and a toilet block at the south end of the footbridge.

This town is the gateway to Drents-Friese Wold Nationaal Park, a beautiful forest area with sand dunes, moors and fens, made for walking and cycling. For a brief visit to the park (less than 2km) go west along the south bank and south on Van Emstweg to the Belvedere tower and the nearby Bosberg sand dunes. Also, ride the signposted Veenwoldsroute (bicycle trail, 43 kilometers), run through the woods and along the Fochtelooërveen, a vast area in which the formation of peat bog continues today.

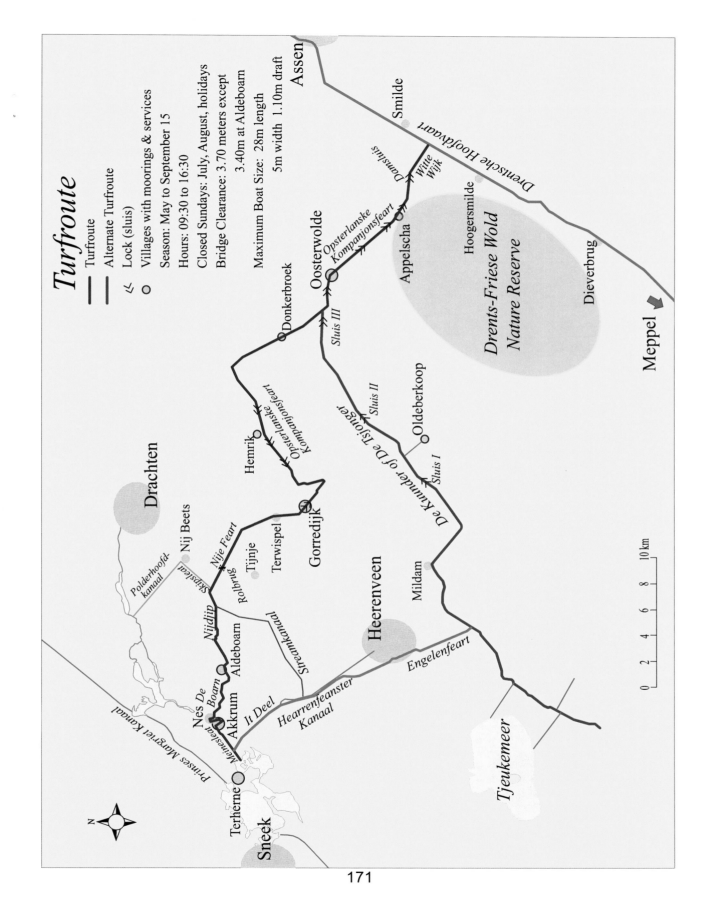

Turfroute

Turfroute
Alternate Turfroute
⌄⌄ Lock (sluis)
○ Villages with moorings & services

Season: May to September 15
Hours: 09:30 to 16:30
Closed Sundays: July, August, holidays
Bridge Clearance: 3.70 meters except
3.40m at Aldeboarn
Maximum Boat Size: 28m length
5m width 1.10m draft

Assen

Smilde

Drentsche Hoofdvaart

Damsluis

Witte Wijk

Opsterlanske Kompanjonsfeart

Oosterwolde

Appelscha

Donkerbroek

Sluis III

Hoogersmilde

Drents-Friese Wold Nature Reserve

Dieverbrug

Meppel

Oldeberkoop

Sluis II

De Kuunder of De Tsjonger

Sluis I

Drachten

Hemrik

Opsterlanske Kompanjonsfeart

Nij Beets

Polderhoofd-kanaal

Skipsleat

Nije Feart

Tijnje

Rolbrug

Terwispel

Gorredijk

Heerenveen

Mildam

Nijdjip

Aldeboarn

Streamkanaal

It Deel

Engelenfeart

Hearrenfeanster Kanaal

Nes De Boarn

Akkrum

Meinesleat

Prinses Margriet Kanaal

Terherne

Sneek

Tjeukemeer

N

0 2 4 6 8 10 km

Turfroute waterways

WATERWAY Names are as shown on ANWB charts	FROM	TO	KM	LOCKS	BRIDGES to open	DEPTH minimum	WIDTH locks/ bridges	HEIGHT fixed bridges	TRAVEL TIME hours
Meinesleat	Terherne	Akkrum	3.5	0	0	1.7	5.3	none	
De Boarn	Akkrum	Aldeboarn	7.5	0	5	1.9	6.0	none	
Nijdjip (Nieuwe Diep)	Aldeboarn	Nije Feart	2.2	0	3	1.7	5.3	3.4	
Nije Feart (Nieuwe Vaart)	Skipsleat	Terwispel	8.2	0	1	1.1	6.0	none	
Opsterlanske Kompanjonsfeart (Opsterlandse Compagnonsvaart)	Terwispel Nije Feart	Gorredijk Verlaat nr.1 sluis	3.1	0	6	1.1	5.3	none	
Opsterlanske Kompanjonsfeart	Gorredijk Verlaat nr.1 sluis	Oosterwolde Sluis III, Tsjonger	19.0	4	20	1.1	5.5	4.0	
Opsterlanske Kompanjonsfeart	Oosterwolde Sluis III, Tsjonger	Appelscha Bovenstverlaat nr. VIII sluis	8.8	3	10	1.1	5.5	3.7	
Witte Wijk	Appelscha Bovenstverlaat nr. VIII sluis	Drentsche Hoofdvaart	5.0	2	6	1.1	5.5	none	
Turfroute	**Terherne to Drentsche Hoofdvaart**		57.3	0	51	1.1	5.3	3.4	20.0
De Kuunder of De Tsjonger	Oosterwolde Sluis III, Tsjonger	Oldeberkoop	11.7	3	1	1.1	5.5	3.7	
Tsjonger	Oldeberkoop	Mildam	9.3						
Tsjonger	Mildam	Engelenvaart	5.5	0	1	1.1	5.1	3.4	
Engelenfeart (Engelenvaart)	Tsonger	Heerenveen	8.7	0	3	1.65	7.0		
Hearrenfeanster Kanaal (Nieuwe Heerenveense Kanaal)	Heerenveen	It Deel	4.6	0	0	2.7	open	none	
It Deel (Het Deel)	Hearrenfeanster	Meinesleat	4.4	0	0	2.2	open	none	
Alternate Turfroute	**Sluis III, Tsjonger to Terherne**		44.2	3	5	1.1	5.1	3.4	8.0

Alternate Turfroute: Tjonger

(The official name in Frisian is Tsjonger; also called Kuinder or Kuunder.)

The Tjonger is essentially a straight-line, uniform-width waterway, but it is not a bit boring. It passes across fields and wetlands for 21 kilometers between Sluis III and Mildam with no parallel highway and only five crossings of country roads. Halfway along the route is an extensive forested section, the Delleburen.

A visit to **Oldeberkoop** is definitely worth it. This typical Drenthe village green is easily reachable by boat from the Tjonger: the canal Preenzewiek leads 800m south to the marina De Uutwiek. The picturesque village of Oldeberkoop is the oldest village in the region. It lies on a sandy ridge between the rivers Linde and Tjonger. The 12th century Romanesque-Gothic church is a must see, as is the forest park near the haven. Oldeberkoop has managed to preserve its rustic character.

Tjonger, Sluis I

Mildam is a small village that has one restaurant to consider: *Hof van Schoterland*
www.hofvanschoterland.nl   0513 63 35 66

De Tjongermolen (left) is a smock mill near Mildam.

Turfroute draaibrug

Footbridges (and some road bridges) in the towns along the Turfroute are *draaibrug* (swinging bridges.) This bridge in Aldeboarn is one of three operated by a bridge watcher.

Some are *zelfbediening*, operated by the boat crew. The bridges turn quite easily, using a handle mounted on the bridge railing. Or it may be done by local youth, for a small tip.

Drenthe Province

The Drentsche Hoofdvaart is the "main highway" from Groningen to Meppel/Zwartsluis and the waterways of central Holland, but skippers should also consider cruising in eastern Netherlands or on into Germany, either east from Meppel or southeast from Groningen.

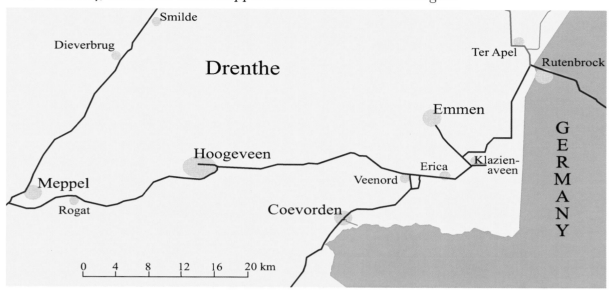

In the past decade the waterways along the German border, surrounding Klazienaveen, have been improved and are now promoted for visitors on the website veenvaart.nl with full details of the routes and the area. The waterways are now suitable for boats 28m long, 4.8m wide, 3.50m high and 1.50m draft (summer) - 1.30m draft (winter). Speed limit is 6 km/hr. Download the magazine Vaar from the website; it is in Dutch but includes useful data tables and photos.

Drenthe Waterways

WATERWAY Names are as shown on ANWB charts	FROM	TO	KM	LOCKS	BRIDGES to open	DEPTH minimum	WIDTH locks/ bridges	HEIGHT fixed bridges	TRAVEL TIME hours
Hoogeveensche Vaart	Meppel Meppeler Diep	Hoogeveen	28.2	3	4	2.5	6.5	5.6	
Verlengde Hoogeveensche Vaart	Hoogeveen	Veenoord	24.6	1	18	2.1	6.2	5.2	
Verlengde Hoogeveensche Vaart	Veenoord	Klazienaveen	9.0	1	4	2.5	6.8	5.6	
Oranjekanaal / Bladderwijk	Klazienaveen	Kon. Willem Alexanderkanaal	1.5	1	0	1.65	6.0	4.6	
Kon. Willem Alexanderkanaal	Oranjekanaal / Bladderwijk	Scholtenskanaal / Sint Josefvaart	2.9	2	0	1.5	6.0	3.8	
Scholtenskanaal / Sint Josefvaart	Kon. Willem Alexanderkanaal	Oosterdiep Compascumkanaal	11.3	1	2	1.5	6.0	3.7	
Oosterdiep Compascumkanaal	Sint Josefvaart	Emmer-Compascuum	9.9	2	3	1.5	6.0	open	
Stads-Compascumkanaal	Emmer-Compascuum	Haren-Rutenbrock Kanaal	5.2	1	8	1.5	6.0	open	
Haren-Rutenbrock Kanaal	Stads-Compascumkanaal	Haren DE	14.0	5	10	1.5	6.0	5.0	
Meppel NL to Haren DE			106.6	17	49	1.5	6.0	3.7	20.0

NETHERLANDS
WINTERSTALLING

--- Canals
--- Rivers
--- Waterways less than
    D=1.5m H=3.5m
(A) Boatyards offering
    Winter Storage

Winterstalling (or *winterberging*)
is the Dutch term for winter storage
of boats. This map and the table on
the next page show just a few of the
boatyards in NL which offer storage
in-water, on land outdoor or indoor
and sometimes indoor heated.
Confirm details, rates and availability
through direct contact with the yard.

Waddenzee

Emden

Delfzijl

Franeker
Harlingen
Leeuwarden
Groningen

(K)
(T) (J)
Bolsward   Grou
Sneek   (I)
(H)
Joure   Heerenveen
Assen

Stavoren
Lemmer

Den Helder

Schagen
Medemblik

IJsselmeer

Steenwijk
Emmen
Rutenbrock (Q)

Enkhuizen
Blokzijl
(L)
Meppel
(S)
Hoogeveen
Coevorden

Hoorn
Urk
Ketelhaven
(M) Zwartsluis
Ommen

Alkmaar (G)
Markermeer
Edam
Kampen

Lelystad
(N) Hattem Zwolle
Elburg

IJmuiden
Haarlem
Harderwijk
Raalte
Almelo

Naarden
Nijkerk
Deventer
Hengelo
Enschede

North Sea
(E)   (F)
Amersfoort
Zutphen

Leiden
Utrecht
Arnhem
Doesburg
Doetinchem

Den Haag
Alphen
a/d Rijn
(R)

Delft
Gouda

Rotterdam
(P)
Gorinchem
Nijmegen

Brielle
Dordrecht
Alem
(C)

Haringvliet
Bies Bosch
Heusden
's-Hertogenbosch

Willemstad
Hollands Diep
(D)
Geertruidenberg

Volkerak
Zevenbergen
Tilburg

Krammer/Zijpe
Ouden-bosch
Etten-Leur
Breda

Tholen
Roosendaal
Helmond

Middelburg
Oosterschelde
Bergen-op-Zoom
Eindhoven
Venlo

Beringe

Westerschelde
Nederweert

Terneuzen
Weert
Bocholt
(B) Roermond
Maasbracht

Antwerpen

BELGIUM

GERMANY

Gent

N

Maastricht
(A)

0 8 16 24 32 40 km

Boatyards offering winterstalling

WATERWAY	MAP #	TOWN	NAME	BOAT LIFT	REPAIRS	STORAGE	PHONE	WEBSITE
Maas river	A	Maastricht	Maastricht Marina - Pietersplas	no	no	in water	043-3671814	www.maastrichtmarina.com
Maas river	B	Maasbracht	Van der Laan Yachting Harry van der Laan	75 tons - 40 tons traveler	powertrain electrical paint	outdoor indoor heated	0475-466430 06-23472256	www.vanderlaanyachting.nl
Maas river	B	Wessem	Van Kuyk Yachting	30 tons - 47 tons traveler	powertrain electrical paint	outdoor indoor heated	0475-563295	www.vankuykyachting.nl
Maas river	B	Roermond	Jachthaven Het Steel	22 tons traveler	no	outdoor indoor heated	0475-318304	www.steelhaven.nl
Maas river	C	Mookerplas	Jachthaven Eldorado	30 tons traveler	no	outdoor indoor	024-6962366	www.eldorado-mook.nl
Amer river	D	Drimmelen	Jachthaven Drimmelen	35 & 75 tons	no	outdoor indoor heated	0162-683935	www.snoek-bovy.nl
Ringvaart van de Haarlemmermeer polder	E	Kudelstaart Westeinder-plas (Aalsmeer)	Kempers Watersport	40 tons	powertrain electrical paint	outdoor indoor in water heated	0297-385385	www.kemperswatersport.nl
Vinkeveense Plassen	F	Vinkeveen	Jachthaven de Wilgenhoek	35 tons	winterizing	outdoor indoor in water	0294-291842	www.de-wilgenhoek.nl
Noordhollandsch kanaal	G	Alkmaar	Jachthaven Witsen	50 tons	powertrain electrical paint	outdoor indoor heated	072-5112297	www.nicolaaswitsen.nl
Ijsselmeer	H	Lemmer	Jachthaven De Punt	?	winterizing	outdoor indoor	0514-563470	www.jachthavendepunt.nl
Houkesloot	I	Sneek	Abma's Jachtwerf	30 tons	powertrain electrical	outdoor indoor in water	0515-419065	www.abma-sneek.nl
Peinder Kanaal	J	Drachten	De Drait Yachting	?	winterizing	outdoor indoor in water	0512-513276	www.jachthavendedrait.nl

Boatyards offering winterstalling

WATERWAY	MAP #	TOWN	NAME	BOAT LIFT	REPAIRS	STORAGE	PHONE	WEBSITE
Van Harinxma Kanaal	K	Leeuwarden	Hemrick Marine	?	no	outdoor indoor heated	058-2880007	www.hemrikmarine.nl
Van Harinxma Kanaal	K	Leeuwarden	Leeuwarder Jachthaven	?	no	outdoor indoor-in water	058-2125759	www.leeuwarderjachthaven.nl
Van Harinxma Kanaal	K	Leeuwarden	Watersport Twee Provinciën	32 tons	winterizing	outdoor indoor-in water	058-2885446	watersporttweeprovincien.nl
Lang Deel/Wartens	K	Wartena	Jachtwerf W. Bijlsma	35 tons	powertrain electrical paint	outdoor indoor in water	058-2550608	www.wbijlsma.nl
Steenwijkerdiep	L	Steenwijk	Jachthaven Steenwijkerdiep	30 tons	no	outdoor indoor in water	0521-520400	www.jachthavensteenwijkerdiep.nl
Meppelerdiep & Zwarte Water	M	Zwartsluis	Jachthaven De Kranerweerd	40 tons	powertrain electrical paint	outdoor indoor heated	038-3867351	www.kranerweerd.nl
Randmeren	N	Elburg	Jachtcenter Elburg	?	winterizing	outdoor indoor heated	052-5682800	www.jachtcenter.nl
Linge	P	Geldermalsen	Conavroegh bv	15 tons	powertrain electrical paint	outdoor indoor	034-5571347	www.conavroegh.nl
Musselkanaal	Q	Ter Apel	Jachthaven de Runde	15 tons	winterizing	outdoor indoor	059-9850953	www.jachthaventerapel.nl
Hollandse Ijssel	R	Ijsselstein	Jachthaven Marnemoende	23 tons	winterizing paint	outdoor indoor	030-6060663	marnemoende.nl
Meppelerdiep	S	Meppel	Jachthaven Meppel	15 tons	powertrain electrical paint	outdoor indoor	052-2258113	www.jachthavenmeppel.nl
Alde Feanen	T	Earnewald	Jachthaven Westerdijk	20 tons	winterizing	outdoor	051-1539360	www.jachthavenwesterdijk.nl

Tutorial: Clearance under bridges

Probably the most important item of data on the charts is bridge height; but it is also the most variable, because clearance will vary as the water level varies. The photo below offers a good example; it is at the town of Mook, over the canal leading from the Maas river into the Mookerplas, home of a popular stopover when traveling the Maas. The fixed bridge happens to be adjacent to a floodgate, which is normally left open.

But what is of interest is the yellow/black scale on the right side; it shows the clearance under the bridge, height in meters. On the chart this bridge is reported as H54, or 5.4 meters clearance. On the day of the photo the water level has in fact exceeded the lower end of the scale; height is estimated to be a bit more than 5.5m.

Mook, brug in de Cuykse Steeg

Screenshots from information sources and a quick method to calculate the actual clearance for this bridge are shown on the next pages.

Chart references are from the Waterkaarten app, described on page 22 of this book.

Daily water level data is from Rijkswaterstaat Waterinfo at: https://waterinfo.rws.nl

Waterinfo

Water levels are displayed and updated daily at: https://waterinfo.rws.nl Take a look at that website and select Waterbeheer; a screenshot is shown below. The green dots are at locations where water level is monitored. A few numbers are shown, more will appear as you zoom in. Green dots are normal level, the ruby dots are low water (Verlaagde waterstand.) The numbers are in centimeters, above or below the NAP zero at Amsterdam. The range of elevation of the water (and also the land, of course) is obvious, it is below NAP around the IJsselmeer and rising in the east and south.

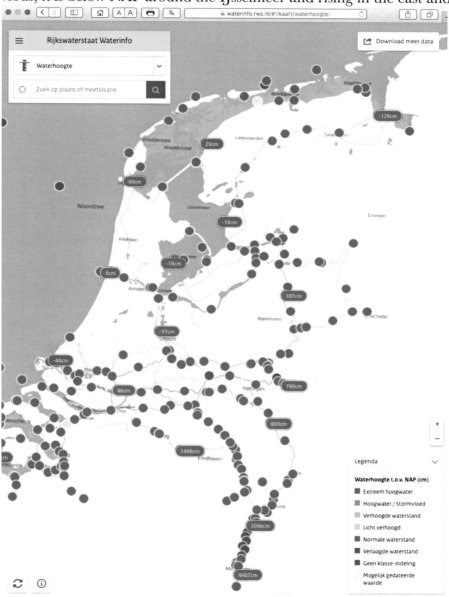

You can see that there are little or no data points for most of the canals within Zuid Holland, Noord Holland, Flevoland, Friesland and Drenthe provinces. Those waterways are canals and small rivers, some within the dikes of polders, which are maintained at fixed level by constant water management. Rivers must be referenced to NAP because the water level can vary significantly. Canals also vary at times, but the operators can adjust the level as needed. The actual level does not vary much and thus "Maximum Clearance" stated on the chart can be trusted.

Waterinfo data

The data point near Mook is in the center of the chart below, on the Maas river: 798cm, or 7.98 meters. 798cm is in the middle of the normal range for that point of 775 to 820cm.

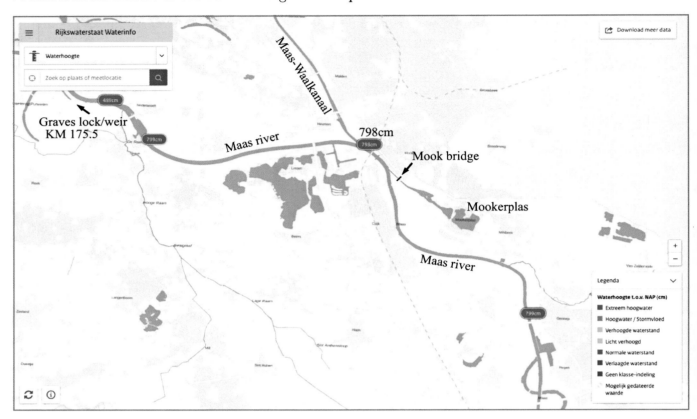

Click (when online at the link at top of this page) on the green oval and then Meer details for a chart showing the trend over previous and future days, along with standard measurements for normal, low or high water.

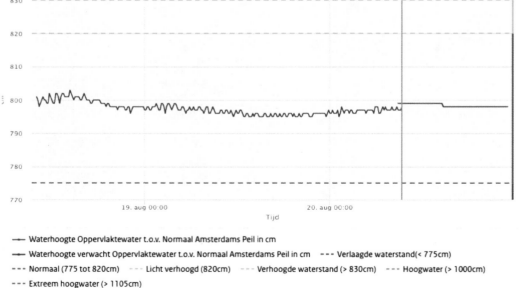

Waterkaarten chart example

The chart data for this bridge states that "Maximum Clearance" is 5.4 meters. It might be better labeled as "Normal Clearance", as both the scale in the photo and the published data show more clearance than the stated maximum.

The "Notes" section of the "More" box offers a way to determine the actual clearance precisely, using the reference to NAP (Normaal Amsterdams Peil.) This measurement is used extensively in eastern and southeastern areas of the Netherlands, where elevation is well above sea level. In this case the bridge height is NAP +13.50m; that is the height of the underside of the bridge above a zero point at Amsterdam. But the skipper doesn't care about that, he/she needs to know the height above the surface of the water, at this point, today. The next pages will show how to find that data and use it in practice.

"Notes" also shows Hoogte (height) SP+6m; SP (Stuwpeil) means weir level, the elevation of the next weir downstream, in this case at Graves lock, where SP Grave = NAP +75dm. The underside of the bridge is 6m above the top of that weir, thus 7.5m + 6m = 13.50m.
Drempeldiepte (threshold depth) of the floodgate adjacent to this bridge is SP-3.50m or NAP+4.00m.

KP (Kanalpeil) is a term used in some areas (but not shown in this example.) It is a local reference level for a specific canal; it can be used to determine clearance height as above, with KP as a substitute for NAP. It is not commonly seen in the Waterkaarten chart, as it is a redundant term; in most cases the clearance is simply stated alone, not referenced to KP. There is no number recorded as the value for the KP of a specific canal. KP is in fact the actual surface level of the water in the canal, which the local operators maintain at or near a constant level. That is why it is seen only in the data for a canal, not a river.

Clearance calculation

The diagram below brings together the measurements described on the previous pages.

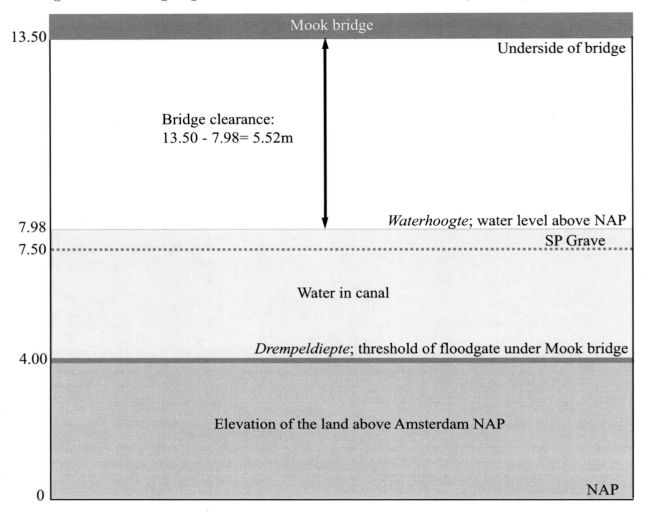

Summary of the terms: NAP (Normaal Amsterdams Peil) = 0

SP (Stuwpeil) = NAP +XXdm = top of downstream weir

KP (Kanaalpeil) = local water level in a specific canal

Conclusion: This tutorial was researched to satisfy the curiosity of the author regarding NAP. In practice, the height stated on the chart can be used with confidence and all of this is moot!

NAP - Normaal Amsterdams Peil

NAP is the reference level to which height (elevation) measurements in the Netherlands are related. It is not sea level, although it is actually close to that reference level. Historically it was measured in the period September 1, 1683-1684 as the average summer flood level of the river IJ. The drawing below show NAP level in blue, with no dikes or polders yet built.

The NAP network consists of approximately 35,000 visible reference marks, usually bronze bolts with the inscription NAP, placed in quays, walls, buildings or on piles throughout the country.
See the website: https://www.normaalamsterdamspeil.nl/en

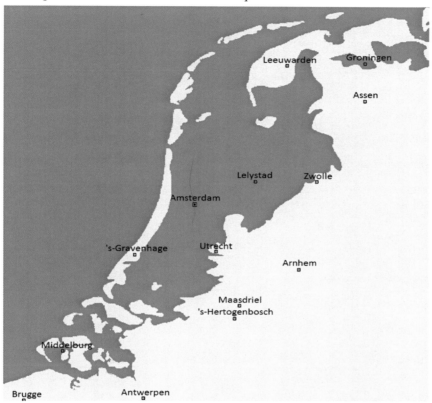

NAP levels are displayed on two floors in the CityHall (Stopera) at the northern end of the Amstel river, on the Waterlooplein.

The NAP zero-point is marked by the red arrow at right, in the lower level of the building. The square column in the foreground has been driven down to a point which keeps it stable. On top of the column is a bronze plaque, which is the precise zero level of NAP. Amsterdam's canals are normally 40cm below NAP.

Glossary of Dutch Boating Terms

Although English is widely spoken in The Netherlands, it is not universal. You will often need to translate phrases on signs, maps and brochures. You won't find some of these words in a Dutch-English dictionary, or online translators. On these pages you will find a table of Dutch terms as related to operating or buying a vessel in The Netherlands.

Note: the letters ij/IJ are pronounced as I (eye) and are listed alphabetically as if they were the letter Y.

Aak	a type of Dutch barge	brandstof	fuel
aanbod	offer, list of boats for sale	brandstoftank	fuel tank size
aankoop	purchase, acquisition	breedte	beam, width
aanlegplaats	mooring place	brug/bruggen	bridge/bridges
achter/achterschip	aft	BTW	VAT (Value Added Tax)
achtersteven	stern	buitenboordmotor	outboard motor
afgesloten	locked	buitenhaven	outer harbor
afmeer	mooring	bijboot, jol	dinghy
afval	rubbish disposal bins	bijzonderheden	particulars, details
algemeen	general	Cadastre/Kadaster	register of ships
aluminium	aluminum	casco	bare hull, no interior structure
anker	anchor	centrale verwarming	central heating
ankerlier	anchor winch	deckshuit	barge
ankerplaats	anchorage	diepgang	draft (water draft)
bakboord	port (left) side	diepte	depth
batterij	battery	dieptemeter	depthsounder
bediening	opening hours schedule	dieselmotor	diesel motor
beneden	lower	dieselolie, gasoil	diesel fuel
benzinemotor	gas (petrol) engine	doorvaart	passageway
bereikbaarheid	how to get there	doorvaarthoogthe	clearance above water
bereops	professional (ship)	douche	shower
besturing	steering	draaiuren	engine hours
betalen	pay	draaibrug	swing bridge
Beurtschip	a type of Dutch barge	drinkwater	drinking water
beweegbare brug BB	Bascule bridge, lifting bridge	fiets	bicycle
bezoekers	visitors	fietspad	cycling path
binnenhaven	inner harbor	fietsverhuur	bicycles for hire
binnenwateren	inland waterways	gat/geul	channel for navigation
binnenboordmotor	inboard motor	geen	no, forbidden
binnenvaartschip	barge, inland waterways ship	geld	money, fee
boeg	bow	gemeente	government, municipal
boegschroef	bowthruster	getuigschrift	certificate of competence
boot	boat	gesloten	closed
bouwer	builder	gracht	canal
bouwjaar	year of construction	haven	harbor
boven	upper	havenmeester	harbormaster

Dutch	English	Dutch	English
hefbrug	vertical-lift bridge	omvormer	converter, inverter
helmstok	tiller	onbekend	unknown
het	the	onder voorbehoud	under contract (to sell)
hefbrug	vertical-lift bridge	ondiep	shallow
helmstok	tiller	oost	east
het	the	open	open
hoogte	height	openingstijden	open hours
houtbouw	wood construction	ophaalbrug	overhead-lever bridge
hutten	cabins	overig	other
inhalen	to overtake, pass	paardekracht (pk)	horsepower
jacht	yacht	passantenhaven	visitor's moorings
jachtbemiddeling	boat broker	platbodem	flat-bottom boat
jachtbouw	boat builder	polyester/GRP	fiberglass
jachtbouwbedrijf	boat builder	prijslist	price list
jachthaven	yacht harbor, marina	registratiehaven	home port
jachtmakelaar	boat broker	reparatie	repairs
jachtmakelaardij	boat brokerage	roer	rudder
jachtwerf	boatyard, service/repair	romp	hull
kaarten	charts	rondbodem	round-bottom boat
kade	pier	rondvaartboten	(round-trip) tour boats
kanaal	canal	ruimteboot	houseboat
kantoor	office	scheepsnaam	boat name
keersluis	flood gates, normally open	scheepspapieren	ship's papers
kiel	keel	scheepswerf	boatyard, service/repair
klimatiseren	air conditioned	scheepstechniek	service/repair
koeling	cooling	schroefas	propellor shaft
koelkast	refrigerator	singel	moat canal
ladder	ladder	slaapplaatsen	sleeping places
lengte	length	sleepboot	tug
lenspomp	bilge pump	sluis/sluizen	lock/locks
ligeld	mooring fee	smeer	grease
ligging	location	snelheid	speed
lichten	lights	spoorbrug	railway bridge
logboek	logbook	staal	steel
Luxemotor	a type of Dutch barge	stahoogte	interior height
marifoon	VHF radio	steiger	mooring pontoon
meld..., melden	report to ...	stroom	electric current
meren	moor	stuurboord	starboard (right) side
merk	marque, make	2e stuurstand	2nd steering position (exterior)
motorjacht	motoryacht	tankstation	fuel station
motorzeiljacht	motorsailer	te koop	for sale
nautofoon	horn	te huur	for hire, for rent
nieuwe	new	Tjalk	a type of Dutch barge
noord	north	touw	rope
occasion	second-hand, opportunity	uit het water halen	haul out
omschrijving	description	vaarbewijs	operator's license
		vaarwater	channel

vast brug	fixed bridge	woonark	houseboat
veer	ferry	woonschip	houseboat
veerpont	pontoon bridge	WSV/WV	water sport (yacht) club
verboden	forbidden	xhroef	propeller
verbruik	fuel consumption	zeilboot	sailboat
verhuur	for hire, for rent	zijkanalen	branch canals
verkocht	sold	zonnepaneel	solar panel
verkoop	for sale	zuid	south
vermogen	motor horsepower		
verval	rise/fall in lock		
verwarming	heating		
verzekering	insurance		
vorm	hull shape		
vriezer	freezer		
vrij	free		
vuilwatertank	holding tank (wastewater)		
VVV	tourist office		
waarschuwing	warning		
walstroom	shore power		
walstroomaansluiting	shore connection		
wasserette	launderette		
waterdruksysteem	pressurized water system		
waterstand	water level		
waterverplaatsing	displacement weight		
WC	toilet		
werf/werven	boatyard		
west	west		
winkel	shop		
winterberging	winter storage		

INDEX

INDEX

INDEX

INDEX

INDEX

More EuroCanals Guides for NL

Orion - A Canal & River Cruise through Holland (Printed Book)

A diary with photos, maps and sketches detailing a 90-day cruise through all twelve provinces of the Netherlands, from Vlissingen in the far southwest corner to Maastricht in the southeastern corner. An extensive section describes a five-day visit to Amsterdam and a thorough exploration of the Heart of Holland (see below.)

The book provides suggested routes and sightseeing locations, along with the details of finding overnight stops and negotiating both locks and the bridges over the waterways. It is an essential handbook for those making a journey through the entire country or a short cruise in just one province.

Cruising the Heart of Holland (Printed Book)

The "Heart of Holland" is the region of lakes, rivers, canals and natural areas within the loop of cities of the *Randstad* – Rotterdam, Delft, Den Haag, Leiden, Haarlem, Amsterdam, Weesp, Hilversum, Utrecht, and Gouda. This book focuses on that region by providing more detail and photos than can be included in the overall Netherlands guide.

North Sea to Germany (PDF Download)

This EuroCanals PhotoNav Guide shows a route between Vlissingen and the Germany border in maps, data tables and photos. The trip begins in Zeeland, through southwestern Netherlands then across the center of the country on the Waal river and into Germany on the Rhein.

EuroCanals Guides

Online Library - Downloads - Books
Go To: www.eurocanals.com

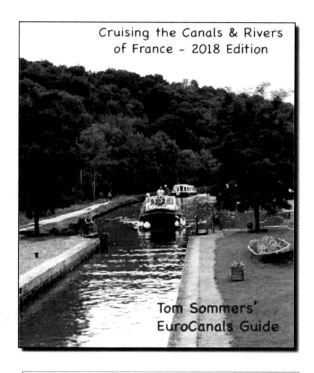

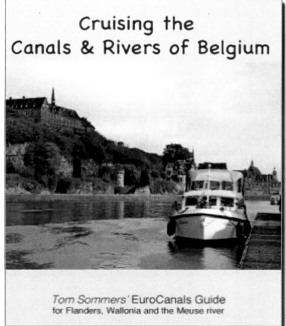

EuroCanals Guides Online Library

Currently 26 guides for pdf download; Subscribe for access to all guides or download each guide individually.

Made in United States
North Haven, CT
05 October 2021